WESTERN CANADA 1909

WILHELM COHNSTAEDT

WESTERN CANADA 1909

TRAVEL LETTERS BY WILHELM COHNSTAEDT

---

translated by HERTA HOLLE-SCHERER
editor, KLAUS H. BURMEISTER

CANADIAN PLAINS STUDIES ■ 7
L. G. CROSSMAN, GENERAL EDITOR OF OCCASIONAL PUBLICATIONS

CANADIAN PLAINS RESEARCH CENTER
UNIVERSITY OF REGINA
1976

ISSN 0317-6290
ISBN 0-88977-003-4

Canadian Cataloguing in Publication Data

Cohnstaedt, Wilhelm, 1880-1937.
Western Canada 1909

(Canadian plains studies ; 7 ISSN 0317-6290)
Translation of Aus Westkanada : Reisebriefe unseres Spezial-dt-Korrespondenten.
ISBN 0-88977-003-4

1. Cohnstaedt, Wilhelm, 1880-1937. 2. The West, Canadian - Description and travel - 1900-1950.* I. University of Regina. Canadian Plains Research Center. II. Title. III. Series.
FC3205.3.C6413 917.12'04'2 C77-002017-8
F1015.C6413

Canadian Plains Research Center
University of Regina
Regina, Saskatchewan
S4S 0A2

Printed and Bound in Canada by Modern Press, Saskatoon.

EDITOR'S NOTE

I gratefully acknowledge a number of institutions, agencies and individuals who have helped to bring this project to fruition. In particular, I wish to thank the Department of the Secretary of State, Ottawa, for a publication grant-in-aid and the Regina Multicultural Council whose sponsorship of this enterprise reflects an increasing public awareness of the ethno-cultural heritage of the Canadian West.

I should also like to express my appreciation to the University of Regina for additional financial assistance, to the Saskatchewan Archives Board, Regina, for the use of pictorial material, and to the Canadian Plains Research Center, University of Regina, for accepting this book in its publication series.

The Travel Letters were first published in 1909 in the *Frankfurter Zeitung*. Translation and publication in Canada was made possible with the kind permission of Verlagshaus Frankfurter Societaets-Druckerei, G.m.b.H., Frankfurt am Main.

Finally, of the many individuals who have supported this project with their continual interest, I am particularly indebted to Dr. L. G. Crossman whose expertise in various areas germane to this publication has greatly aided our task.

Klaus H. Burmeister
University of Regina

TRANSLATOR'S NOTE

A great deal of time and research has gone into the translation of this book which was given to me by Joy and Martin Cohnstaedt several years ago. The content, consisting of eleven chapters of widely varying length, appeared between October 10 and December 12, 1909 as a newspaper series in the *Frankfurter Zeitung* (though Chapter 11 could possibly have been added later). Shortly after, the eleven chapters were published in book form by the Frankfurter Societäts-Druckerei, G.m.b.H., under the title of *Aus Westkanada, Reisebriefe unseres Spezial-dt-Korrespondenten (From Western Canada, Travel Letters from our special correspondent),* and this small book has served as the material for the translation from the German. The text has been translated complete and unabridged.

Considering this document a kind of legacy, I have taken great pains to retain Wilhelm Cohnstaedt's very distinct style, although it is in places somewhat long-winded and interspersed with references to the classics and things Germanic-Romantic, in keeping with the literary fashion of the time. The occasional change in his style — from the perceptive, beautifully descriptive, sometimes humorous-sarcastic, very polished, to the staccato sentences reminiscent of a telegraphic message — can obviously be explained by the fact that he was restricted, to a varying degree, by stringent deadlines. Further, one must keep in mind that he had to cover an extremely vast area in a very short time, travelling by train, with an occasional side trip on horseback or by horse-drawn coach, but never too far away from the railway track, a fact which determined his choice of topical reports: he concentrated either on the major centres of the new land, or on items that carried a certain amount of healthy sensationalism for the waiting public back home.

In the translation, his often unusual but very graphic imagery has been purposely retained; cognates have been used as much as possible. There are no footnotes; instead, explanatory notes are provided between square brackets where they seem necessary. If there was a choice, the terminology — especially in agricultural matters — is that used on the prairies. Every effort has been made to let the style of the author, not that of the translator, come through. In short, it is hoped that this translation is a true reflection of what the eminent journalist put down on paper near the end of the first decade of this century.

My special thanks go to Glenda Galvin, Librarian of Campion College, for spending considerable time with me going over the translation and for making many valuable suggestions.

Herta Holle-Scherer
University of Regina

TABLE OF CONTENTS

Chapter

Nr. 281. Viertes Morgenblatt. Vierundfünfzigster Jahrgang **Sonntag, 10. Oktober 1909.**

Abonnementspreis:
Ein Viertelj. in Frankfurt u. Mainz a. d. Exp. ℳ 7.50, b. d. Agent. ℳ 8.25, a. d. Postamt. in Deutschland ℳ 9.- Aegypten Milliémes 737, Belgien Fr. 13.92, Bulgarien Fr. 20.70, Dänemark Kr. 9.96, Griechenland (durch d. Postamt in Triest) Kr. 19.90, Holland fl. 7.20, Italien Fr. 15.10, Luxemburg Fr. 13.05, Marokko (D.P.) Pes. 18.93, Norwegen Kr. 9.59, Oesterreich (Wien auch Wollzeile 11) Kr. 15.54, Portugal Milr. 3.650, Rumänien Lei 16.30, Russland Rbl. 4.53, Schweden Kr. 10.32, Schweiz Fr. 13.70, Serbien Fr. 14.63, Türkei (D.P.) ℳ 14.34, Ungarn Kr. 12.42, im Weltpostverein, in London Siegle, 30 Lime Str., Paris Agence Havas, New-York 20 Broad Str., sämtlich ℳ 18.—.

Frankfurter Zeitung

und Handelsblatt.

(Frankfurter Handelszeitung.) (Neue Frankfurter Zeitung.)

Begründet von Leopold Sonnemann.

Preis der Anzeigen:
Colonelzeile 45 ₰, Abendbl. 60 ₰, Reklamen ℳ 2.—, Platz- u. Datenvorschriften ohne Verbindlichkeit. — Anzeigen nehmen an: Unsere Expeditionen in: Frankfurt a. M., Gr. Eschenheimerstr. 33/37, Mainz: Schillerpl. 3, Berlin: Leipz. Pl. 3, Dresden-Laubegast: Poststr. 3, München: Theatinerst. 44, Offenbach: Bieberstr. 34, Stuttgart: Langestr. 1. Unsere übrig. Agentur. u. d. Annoncen-Exp. Ferner in: London: 14/18 Queen Victoriastreet. Paris: Agence Havas und John F. Jones & Co., Zürich: Nordstrasse 62, Brüssel: 1 Rue de la Blanchisserie, New-York: 20 Broad Street. Verlag und Druck der Frankfurter Societäts-Druckerei (Gesellschaft m. beschr. Haftung)

Aus Westkanada.

(Von unserem Spezialkorrespondenten)

I.

Winnipeg und Brandon.

dt Calgary (Alberta), im August.

„Vieles Gewaltige gibt es, und nichts ist gewaltiger als der Mensch!"

Hier habe ich Halt gemacht, am Westrande der ungeheuren Ebene zwischen den Großen Seen und dem Felsengebirge, um zu erzählen, was ich in diesem Lande gesehen habe. Aber bevor ich zum Schreiben mich niedersetze, werden die Streifbänder aufgerissen, die Nummer vom 1. August herausgesucht und zwei Artikel verschlungen: „Die Zeppelinfahrt zur Ila" und „Zeppelin in Frankfurt". Niemand kann ein großes Erlebnis stärker mitempfinden, als wer selbst soeben Großes erlebt hat. Mir wars nicht vergönnt, den Helden vom Bodensee die Luft bezwingen zu sehen, aber ich sah den Menschen die Wildnis der Erde bezwingen, und keinen besseren Spruch könnte ich mir wählen als das Antigonewort, mit dem der Frankfurter Stadtvorstand den Grafen gegrüßt hat: „Vieles Gewaltige gibt es, und nichts ist gewaltiger als der Mensch!"

Vieles Gewaltige habe ich hier gesehen, unterm Zauberstab hochgeschossene Städte, große und kleine, alle monumental, über die unendliche Prairie bin ich dahingefahren im Dampfwagen, in der Kutsche und auf Pferderücken, sah die Rocky Mountains zum ersten Male und bin in das erste Indianerkamp hinabgeritten: wie schwindet das alles in nichts vor dem einen großen Erlebnis, wie des Menschen Wissen und Geist ein Land lebendig macht, das vor wenig Jahren noch als ungastlich, unwirtlich und unnütz galt.

In **Winnipeg** habe ich den Boden Westkanadas betreten, aber man kann nicht von Winnipeg berichten ohne das Land gesehen zu haben, dessen Ausfluß es ist. Hier wachsen die ersten historischen Kapitel einer neuen Nationalwirtschaft vor unseren Augen. Da ist die Stadt noch kein Wesen an sich. Sie ist nur Konsequenz des Ackerbaues. Gehört zu seinen Arbeitsmitteln, in einer Reihe mit Pflug und Dreschmaschine und mit der Molkerei. Sie ist wie das Kontor einer großen Fabrik; Verkaufszentrale und Einkaufszentrale. Man hat den kanadischen Westen mit einer dickbauchigen Flasche verglichen, deren enger Hals zwischen den Seen Manitobas auf der einen und den Großen Seen sowie der Grenze der Ver- für das in sicherer Aussicht stehende kanadische Minneapolis von 300 000, sondern für die erwartete Millionenstadt, das kanadische Chicago. Der Besucher denkt lächelnd an das kleine Karlchen, da es mit Vaters Gehrock und Zylinder sich kostümierte. Aber dies ist mehr als komische Maskerade. Wer mit den Menschen spricht in den Läden, den Kontoren, der Verwaltung, wer über das Werden hinaussieht auf das, was wird, der überzeugt sich, Winnipeg weiß, was es tut, und wird in den heute noch etwas komisch schlotternden Rock hineinwachsen. Die Einwohnerzahl dieser Stadt betrug 1871: 241; 1881: 7900; 1891: 25 600; 1901: 42 300 und heute bei vorsichtigster Schätzung: 125 000. Die Perioden des großen Wachstums waren das vorletzte Jahrzehnt des alten und das erste des neuen Jahrhunderts, genau entsprechend den Siedlungsperioden der westkanadischen Prairie. Um die Wende von 1880 brachten Bau und Vollendung der Canadian Pacific Railway den ersten großen Einwandererstrom, und in den letztvergangenen Jahren kam gleichzeitig über den Atlantik und aus den Vereinigten Staaten ein Massenstoß, der jene erste Periode weit hinter sich ließ. Man hat mir erzählt, daß erst seit etwa zehn Jahren die Häuser Winnipegs mit festen Fundamenten gebaut werden, weil erst seitdem alle Zweifel an der dauernden und allgemeinen Besiedelung Westkanadas geschwunden sind. Nach der Fahrt durch die drei Prairieprovinzen, Manitoba, Saskatchewan und Alberta, unter dem Eindruck dessen, was da kolonisatorisch geleistet wird und geleistet werden kann, sehe ich in der Prophezeiung und dem Ziele „Winnipeg, das Chicago Kanadas" mehr als eitel Großsprecherei.

Die Detailgeschäfte sind das, was dem Fremden zuerst in die Augen springt. Sie sind natürlich nicht das, was die Bedeutung einer Stadt wie Winnipeg ausmacht. Die Funktion der Einkaufsstelle und Verteilungszentrale für den ganzen Nordwesten erfüllt der Großhandel Winnipegs, der bereits heute einen imponierenden Umfang aufweist. Die beiden Warenhäuser der Stadt stehen gleichzeitig an der Spitze des Großhandels. Da ist zuerst die **Hudson Bay Co.**, die man aus der Geschichte als einstige Herrin des ganzen Landes zwischen Hudson Bay, Eismeer und Pacific kennt, eines Landes, annähernd so groß wie Europa, und die man nun als Warenhaus wieder findet. Das berührt anfangs als tragische Dekadenz, aber in Wirklichkeit ist es der Gesellschaft nicht schlecht ergangen. Nach einer Dauer von 180 Jahren wurde ihre Herrschaft 1860 durch eine große Geldzahlung und die anderes mehr oder weniger wildes Getier unterhält. Auch ein Karussel fehlt nicht. Tiergarten und Vergnügungspark: so schafft die Straßenbahn sich selbst den Verkehr, der ihr zum Leben und Verdienen unentbehrlich ist. Sie handelt damit genau nach dem Muster der großen amerikanischen Bahngesellschaften, die nicht warten, bis Fracht und Passagiere zu ihnen kommen, sondern sie herbeiholen und das Land, durch das sie hindurchfahren, systematisch kolonisieren.

Das bedeutendste Beispiel eines solchen wahrhaft produktiven Verkehrsunternehmens hat man gerade hier in Winnipeg mit der Canadian Pacific Railway, die wohl überhaupt die größte private Transportanstalt der Welt ist. Man fragt sich hier bald, was gehört der C. P. R. eigentlich nicht? Am Bahnhof der C. P. R. komme ich an, und das Hotel, nach dem ich mich begebe, steht im Besitz und Betrieb der C. P. R. Der erste Wagen, der auf der Straße an mir vorbeifährt, prunkt mit der Inschrift „C. P. R. Dampfwäscherei" und, um eine Drahtnachricht abzusenden, werde ich zum Telegraphenbureau der C. P. R. gewiesen. Die C. P. R, mit ihren direkten Untergesellschaften, hat gegenwärtig eine Schienenlänge von 22 500 km, sie betreibt die größten Schnelldampferlinien zwischen Kanada und England, Kanada und Australien, Kanada und Ostasien, daneben den Schiffsverkehr von Vancouver nordwärts und südwärts an der pazifischen Küste entlang und ihre eigenen Dampfer über die Großen Seen, sie betreibt vierzehn der größten und modernsten Hotels über ganz Kanada hin. Die C. P. R. ist wohl auch eine der größten Landgesellschaften, da sie heute noch vier Millionen Hektar zu verkaufen hat; von ihrer kolonisatorischen Tätigkeit werde ich später erzählen.

Wer von Winnipeg mit der C. P. R. nach Westen fährt, der erwartet, gleich hinter der Stadt in das gelobte Land der „unübersehbaren" Weizenfelder einzutreten. Die Erwartung wird getäuscht. Man sieht anfangs recht viel unkultivierte Prairie, später wieder ganze Strecken steinigen Buschlandes, dazwischen Felder, doch nicht viel größer, als wir sie in Deutschland gewohnt sind, meist Weizen und Hafer, daneben Gerste, roter Klee und Luzerne. Dann und wann ein paar weidende Herden, schönes Vieh. Auch die Getreidefelder stehen dicht und gut, wenn auch üppig mit Unkraut durchsetzt. Die prachtvolle Ernte ist das allgemeine Gesprächsthema. Seit ein paar Tagen hat das Schneiden des Weizens begonnen. Hier und dort sehen wir von der Bahn aus den „Binder" arbeiten, die Maschine, die von drei oder vier steht bereits seit 21 Jahren. Ihre Aufgabe ist, zu untersuchen, was alles in dem Klima Westkanadas gebaut werden kann, und welche Methoden hierfür die geeignetsten sind. Heuer wurden beispielsweise zwanzig Varietäten Luzerne gepflanzt, um eine Art zu finden, die der nordischen Kälte standzuhalten vermag. Im allgemeinen liegt die landwirtschaftliche Beschränkung Westkanadas jedoch nicht in der Strenge der kalten Jahreszeit, sondern in ihrer Ausdehnung. Der Sommer dauert in der Regel von Mitte April bis Ende August und muß aufs schärfste genutzt werden, denn für Frühling und Herbst kommen nur wenige Wochen auf jeder Seite hinzu. Der Sommer ist dann allerdings sehr warm und die Verteilung der Niederschläge, meist Juni und Juli außerordentlich günstig. In diesem Jahre wurde es besonders spät, und die Farmer haben deshalb, in allen Teilen Westkanadas, die ich sah, mehr Hafer und etwas weniger Weizen gesät als sie sonst getan hätten. Mitbestimmend war dafür auch der gute Preis des Hafers, der zum Teil auf die vielen Bahnbauten und ihren starken Pferdeverbrauch zurückgeführt wird. Daß die Felder der Versuchsfarm ein besonders schönes Bild bieten, liegt in der Natur ihres Berufes und was eine mehrstündige Rundfahrt von anderen Farmen sehen ließ, deutete auf den guten erzieherischen Einfluß des Regierungsunternehmens.

Die Betriebsgröße scheint in der Regel 150 bis 400 Hektar zu betragen; das größte Weizenfeld, das ich zu sehen bekam, bedeckte etwa 80 Hektar und stand ausgezeichnet. Ein prachtvolles Bild, wenn der Sommerwind darüber hinfährt und es wiegt und schaukelt wie die sanften Wogen eines Sees. Dem Regierungseinflusse ist es auch zu danken, daß der Farmer sein Heim nicht mehr nackt und kahl mitten in die Prairie hineinsetzt, sondern Bäume pflanzt. Beinahe jedes Haus ist nach Westen und Norden, den Windseiten, von dichten Baumgruppen umgeben, Weißpappeln in der Regel. Die forstliche Versuchsfarm der Dominionregierung in Indian Head, Saskatchewan, versendet diese Bäume umsonst gegen das Versprechen sorgsamer Pflege; die Ausführung des Versprechens wird regelmäßig kontrolliert. Die Prairie war hier wohl nie sehr stark bewaldet, was aber da war, haben die immer wiederholten Waldbrände endgültig ausgerottet. Nur sehr vereinzelt gibt es hier und da noch eine natürliche Baumgruppe. Als wir an einer davon vorbeifahren, springt knapp zehn Schritte vor unserem Wagen ein Prairiewolf heraus, anspruchsloser als Coyote bekannt, und galoppiert in großen

I WINNIPEG AND BRANDON

Calgary (Alberta) in August

"Creation is a marvel and man its masterpiece."
(Sophocles, *Antigone*)

Here at the western edge of the immense plain which stretches from the Great Lakes to the Rocky Mountains I have paused in my journey in order to report what I have seen in this country. But before I sit down to write, I rip open the postal wrapper [around the papers forwarded to me from home], look for the August 1st issue, and devour two articles: "Flight of the Zeppelin to Ila" and "Zeppelin in Frankfurt." Nobody can share the feeling of a great happening more keenly than the person who has just experienced something great himself. I did not have the privilege of seeing the hero of Lake Constance conquer the air, but I have seen man conquer the wilds of the earth; and I myself could have chosen no better quotation than the words from "Antigone" with which the City Council of Frankfurt greeted the Count [i.e., Count Zeppelin]: "Creation is a marvel and man its masterpiece."

I have seen many marvels here — cities sprung up as if touched by magic wand — big cities, small cities, all monumental; I have crossed the endless prairie by steam-train, by coach, and on horseback; I have seen the Rocky Mountains for the first time, and I have ridden into my first Indian encampment. But how all this fades into nothingness before the one great realization of how the knowledge and the spirit of man bring to life a country that, only a few years ago, was considered inhospitable, desolate, and useless!

* * *

I set foot on western Canadian soil in Winnipeg, but one cannot report on Winnipeg without having seen the country whose product it is. Here, the first historic chapters of a new national economy emerge before our very eyes. At this point the city is not yet an entity as such, but only an outgrowth of agriculture. It belongs to its means of production in the same way as the plough, the threshing-machine and the dairy. It is comparable to the office of a great factory; a sales and purchasing centre. The Canadian West has been likened to a big-bellied bottle, whose narrow neck lies between the lakes of Manitoba on the one side, and the Great Lakes and the American border on the other side. In this bottleneck Winnipeg has established itself, and everything has to pass through it — the wheat and the cattle being shipped across the lakes to the east coast and on to Europe; machines, implements, and all the supplies that the young farm-country has to obtain from the outside. The opening at the bottom of the bottle facing British Columbia (which is usually not included in the term "western Canada" or "the Northwest") has so far played only a minor role, and the smaller outlets toward the United States to the west of Winnipeg are of even less importance.

Whoever comes to Winnipeg from St. Paul and Minneapolis, the twin-cities of the American Northwest, cannot help noticing the family resemblance. They, too, are essentially market-places for a huge agricultural area — and considerably older places at that — each one presently being double the size of the newly burgeoning Winnipeg and therefore naturally more urbane and refined. The character of the business streets of all three cities is the same — everything is orientated toward the farmer and his wife who come into the city to buy all the necessities for their house and farm. These people are also prosperous enough, however, to pick up a hat in the "next-to-latest" New York — or the latest Winnipeg — fashion, a Winchester rifle for the man, a fur coat which everybody needs in this northern cold, and finally a new pocket-watch, a brooch, or another piece of jewellery. One notices the large number of jewellery stores in all three cities. Only those in St. Paul, however, show any degree of artistic taste; Winnipeg's are more remarkable for glitter than for taste — in keeping with the youthfulness of the Canadian settlements.

Winnipeg appears less English, perhaps even less Canadian, than the still younger and more westerly cities such as Regina or Calgary. It is THE American city pure and simple. Along Main Street, one or two huge business buildings always alternate in colourful succession with two or three shabby shacks dating back to the early years. A railway station on Main Street, destroyed by fire thirteen years ago, still lies in ruins today, and nobody seems to care. For, just like the typical American city, Winnipeg considers itself primarily a building site and only secondarily a built-up area. It lives entirely in the future. The asphalt roads are extremely wide — far wider than they need to be for the present. One does not build for today's city of 125,000 inhabitants, nor even for the surely foreseeable Canadian Minneapolis of 300,000, but for the projected city of a million, the

Canadian Chicago. With a chuckle, the visitor thinks of little Charlie getting dressed up in Father's tail-coat and top-hat. But this is more than just a comical masquerade. Anyone who talks with the people in the stores, in the offices, in administrative positions — anyone who sees beyond the growing stage of what is to come — is convinced that Winnipeg knows what it is doing, and that it will grow into the rather comically flapping "tail-coat" of today. The number of residents in this city was 241 in 1871, 7,900 in 1881, 25,600 in 1891, 42,300 in 1901; and today [1909] 125,000 would be a most conservative estimate. The periods of great growth were the next-to-last decade of the old century and the first decade of the new one, corresponding exactly to the periods of settlement in the western Canadian prairie. At the end of the 1880's, the construction and the completion of the CPR brought the first great influx of immigrants. In the last few years, leaving the first period far behind, a massive thrust occurred simultaneously from overseas and from the United States. I have been told it was not until a few years ago that houses in Winnipeg were built with a solid foundation. Only since that time have all the doubts about the permanent and general settlement of western Canada disappeared. After travelling across the three prairie provinces (Manitoba, Saskatchewan, and Alberta) impressed by what is and can be achieved in terms of settling the country, I see more than idle boasting in the prediction and the goal: "Winnipeg, the Chicago of Canada."

The retail stores are the first things which catch the stranger's eye. Of course, it is not they that make a city like Winnipeg important. The function of purchasing and distribution centre for the entire Northwest is being filled by Winnipeg's wholesale trade which, as of today, shows impressive scope. Side by side at the top of the wholesale trade are the two department stores in the city. There is first the Hudson's Bay Company, known in history as the one-time mistress of the entire country between Hudson Bay and the Arctic and Pacific Oceans — a country nearly the size of Europe — which one meets again as a department store. At first one thinks of this as a tragic decline, but in reality the Company did not fare badly. In 1860, after a span of 180 years, its supremacy was brought to an end by a large cash settlement and the transfer of substantial real estate to the Company. In the Northwest Territories its trading posts still have practically the same character as in the founding year of 1670; essentially, they are in the fur-trading business. In the settled prairie provinces, the trading posts have become department stores, all of which convey a very solid impression, though they appear, by American standards, to be somewhat too conservative and unassuming. It is said that these retail stores of the Company show little or no profit at all, while the real estate, the wholesale business, and the trading posts in the Territories still are very lucrative. In Winnipeg, of late, the T. Eaton Company of Toronto, the largest department store in Canada, is by far the Bay's stiffest competition. This company employs around 10,000 people in both cities, and, in Winnipeg alone, covers an area of four hectares [one hectare = 2.471 acres]. When such an important and established firm as the T. Eaton Co. erects, in a very young country town, buildings that would suffice for Chicago or Berlin, it must indeed have unusual confidence in the future and growth of the place. This department store, which is being run in the grandest style and by the most modern means, has also developed a huge mail-order business all over the West and has, as mentioned before, a significant wholesale business. A considerable number of industrial firms have set up shop in Winnipeg, but of course they are of much less importance than the trading houses. Besides its role as a distribution centre, the city functions as a central depot for the products of the Northwest. Today, Winnipeg is already the largest, if not the most important, grain market of the British Empire. On the average 200 million bushels of grain are said to have been turned over during the last few years.

The residential streets of Winnipeg already give a much greater impression of harmony than the business centre. Here the width of the streets is pleasantly accentuated by rows of trees and strips of lawn. The houses, too, are surrounded by greenery; all look livable and, in some cases, tasteful. They seem to attest to a prosperity of the people that is quite surprising for a city of this size. The banks of the two rivers, the Red and the Assiniboine, which converge in Winnipeg, offer modest scenic attractions. Strangely enough, the streetcar company has looked after the recreation of the general public: it has turned a sizable wooded area along the Assiniboine into a park and keeps a number of buffalo within great enclosures, and other species of wild animals in adjoining cages. A merry-go-round, an animal park, and an amusement park are there, too. In this way, the tramline itself creates the traffic essential to assure its existence and profits. This is exactly what the big American railroad companies do: they don't wait for freight and passengers to come to them; rather, they get them by systematically settling the country they run through.

Here in Winnipeg, the most important example of such a truly productive transportation company is the CPR, which is probably the largest private carrier in the world. Soon one asks oneself the question: what actually is not CPR property? I arrive at the CPR station; the hotel I head for is owned and operated by the CPR; the first vehicle that drives past me in the streets flaunts the inscription "CPR Steam Laundry"; and to send a wire, I am referred to the CPR Telegraph Office. At the present time the CPR and its immediate subsidiaries own 22,500 kilometres of track; they run the biggest Express Steam Line between Canada and England, Canada and Australia, Canada and East-Asia, as well as the shipping traffic from Vancouver northward and southward along the Pacific Coast and their own steamships on the Great Lakes; they operate fourteen of the largest and most modern hotels all over Canada. Furthermore, the CPR is probably one of the biggest real estate companies, for at the present time it owns four million hectares of salable land. I shall report on its colonization policy later on.

Travelling west from Winnipeg, by CPR, one might expect to enter immediately into the promised land of limitless wheat fields. This expectation is not fulfilled. At first one sees much virgin prairie; later on, stretches of rock-strewn bush country, in between fields no bigger than we are used to in Germany — mostly wheat and oats, but also some barley, red clover, and alfalfa. Here and there one sees grazing herds — beautiful livestock. The fields of grain also stand thick and good, although heavily intergrown with weeds. For some days now the harvesting of the wheat has been in progress. Now and then, from the train, we see the binder at work. This machine, drawn by three or four horses, cuts the crop in a width of two or three metres and throws the ready-bound sheaves to the side. At one point I asked a few farm boys whether they had ever seen somebody work with a scythe. "Sure," one of them said, "the teacher showed us a picture of it"; and another had been told by his grandfather how they had to toil with it in the "old country."

However, when crossing Manitoba in a fast train one gets a thoroughly misleading picture of this province's agriculture. Indeed, even deeper inside the country one will seldom find today the immense wheat fields we have heard so much about. The soil in this oldest of the Canadian prairie provinces is not quite virginal any more. The yields are getting smaller, and the largely superficial land use must be changed. It is becoming a more and more common practice to let the fields lie fallow every third summer, and to cultivate them more thoroughly; now and then an innovator may even venture into rotating the crops. These methods, actually, tend to reduce the fields in size. They also require much more, and more conscientious, work. Farm labourers, however, are an expensive luxury in a colonial country, and increasingly the very large farms seem to be disappearing altogether in western Canada. (Around Brandon the monthly pay for permanent farm-hands is $25 to $30 plus free room and board; for harvest-work, $50 to $60.) That the agricultural picture looks all too unfavourable when viewed from the train can be attributed partly to land speculation which causes valuable stretches along the railway line to lie idle. I gained the impression, nevertheless, that the fields deeper inside the country are kept cleaner and are cultivated more thoroughly.

In Brandon, 200 kilometres west of Winnipeg, I stopped over for a day in order to see a little more of the countryside, and at the same time to visit the experimental and school farm of the Dominion Government there. True, the little town itself has grown from 5,600 to 11,000 inhabitants since 1901, but it appears quieter and more staid, not only than the more westerly places, but also than Winnipeg. Its rural district has been almost completely settled since the Eighties, and mostly by eastern Canadians. Whereas the people in all the other western communities I visited brag only about their growth and all the innovations, the Brandonians boast of the fact that they have settled down and more and more resemble a quiet little town in eastern Canada.

The Experimental Farm on the north bank of the Assiniboine that flows past Brandon comprises about 740 acres and has already been in existence for 21 years. Its task is to test what can be grown in the western

Canadian climate, and which methods are most suitable. This year, for instance, 20 varieties of alfalfa were planted in order to find a strain that can withstand the northern cold. In general, however, the limitation in western Canada for agriculture does not lie in the severity of the cold season but rather in its long duration. As a rule, the summer lasts from the middle of April to the end of August and must be used to the utmost because there are only a few weeks of spring and fall on either side of summer. The summer is very warm, though, and the distribution of rain, mostly in June and July, is extremely favourable. This year, spring came especially late and therefore the farmers, in all parts of western Canada that I have seen, have seeded more oats and somewhat less wheat than they normally would have. Another determining factor for this was the good price of oats, which can be partly explained by the heavy use of horses in the extensive railway construction. The fields of the Experimental Farm offer a beautiful sight — as they are meant to do. What I saw when touring the district for several hours indicated the good influence this government enterprise has educationally on the other farms.

As a rule, the size of a farm seems to be between 150 and 400 hectares; the largest wheat-field I got to see covered around 80 hectares and was an excellent stand. It is a magnificent sight when the summer wind passes over the wheat-field, and it sways and rolls back and forth like the gentle waves of a lake. It is also thanks to the influence of the government that the farmer no longer puts up his home bare and bleak in the middle of the prairie, but plants trees. Nearly every house is sheltered to the west and the north, the windward sides, by thick clusters of trees, usually white poplars. The Forest Experimental Farm of the Dominion Government at Indian Head, Saskatchewan, distributes these trees, free of charge, in exchange for a promise by the farmer to tend the trees carefully. Periodical supervision ensures that this promise is kept. Probably the prairie in this part of the country was never heavily wooded, and whatever had grown here was eradicated by repeated forest fires. Only here and there can a natural clump of trees still be found. As we are driving past one of these, a prairie wolf, more commonly called a coyote, jumps out barely ten feet in front of our carriage and races across the prairie in great leaps. After 200 paces, he stops, watches us, and hurries off only after my guide bombards him with terrible roars. "You see," he says, "you have to hear a coyote howl at least once, so that you don't forget that in spite of all the agricultural development you see here, we are after all driving around in the Wild West." However, the yellow-grey beast shows no interest in my education; and he probably knows anyhow, better than my guide, that according to the precepts of natural science and all the experts, he is only entitled to howl at night.

Courtesy of Saskatchewan Archives

City Hall, Regina

II REGINA

Calgary (Alberta) in August

When you travel from the little country town of Brandon, Manitoba, 360 kilometres westward to Regina, Saskatchewan, a place the size of Brandon, and expect to find a similar little country town, you will have the surprise of your life. Here, asphalt-paved streets lead you to an elegant hotel, noteworthy in that it does not belong to the CPR. You pass by an imposing City Hall that one would normally only expect in a big city and past a post office of sandstone and marble, which is the envy of one of my co-travellers from New York; there are large, almost over-elegant stores, and palatial banks, not to be outdone by the public buildings. Like Brandon and many other western towns, Regina originated in the early Eighties in connection with the construction of the CPR, but for twenty years made as little progress as the rest of the country. Only the stream of immigrants of the last decade made it swell to five times its original size in eight years (i.e., from 2,600 in 1901 to its present 12,000). Regina has, of course, the advantage of being the capital of the Province of Saskatchewan, but this cannot be the essential reason for its growth; after all, it was the seat of the government of the Northwest Territories even before the province was established in 1905. The Regina of today is the product of the agricultural abundance of its surrounding countryside. When it was founded it was named the Queen of the Prairie; today it is the Queen of the Wheat-Country.

On a tour through the rural area surrounding Regina, I notice fields of wheat and oats that are not only larger but also more fertile than those I saw in western Manitoba. Most of them are carefully cultivated. Here and there a small stretch has been hit by hail; but on the whole, crops look uniformly lush and one ends up being nearly intoxicated by them. After all that I have seen of farms and farmers, I am reminded of a comment from Professor [Max] Sering's Book, *The Competition in North American Agriculture* [Leipzig, 1887]. Sering's impression around the mid-Eighties was that the farmers in western Canada managed to make a modest living — but barely so — and that they were, on the whole, no better off than the peasants in western Siberia. How all this has changed now! Occasionally, one sees a farmer drive into the city with his automobile; and in my hotel the room next to mine — an expensive one with bath — is a farmer's permanent city accommodation. Remember these are not estate owners, not landed nobility, not capitalistic entrepreneurs either, these are farmers! Farmers who all started out with very little and often with nothing at all and whose farms today are large according to our standards, but only so large as to require few, if any, hired hands. Most of them are still doing all the ploughing, seeding, and cutting by themselves, and can only take off in the car if their sons are old enough to look after the work.

However, the stories of old-timers who are still around confirm that Sering's impression, in his time, was correct. The first wave of settlers that arrived with the construction of the CPR soon ebbed away. The hope for a new Promised Land seemed to have been cruelly thwarted. Much misfortune and poor yields appeared to be the lot of the indomitable pioneers who would attempt to grow wheat in this northern country. The winters were too severe and lasted too long, the summers neither hot nor wet enough; and before the wheat could ripen, it was killed off by the first frost. Does the Canada of today lie under different stars? Everybody assures me that the summers, for the last decade, have become longer, hotter, and rainier, and that the farmer couldn't wish for a better climate than the one here in western Canada. Actually, there has been some change in the climate, but apparently it is somewhat exaggerated by the general public. In all three provinces the farmers are convinced that the higher temperatures are the direct result of the soil cultivation of the past few years. The experts categorically deny this. It is more reasonable to suppose that soil cultivation is partly responsible for the decrease in dryness. However, the main change probably lies in the fact that, during these years, farmers have learned to adapt the selection of their seed grains and their methods of cultivation to the natural conditions of the land.

In any case, the settlement of Saskatchewan as well as that of Alberta did not start in earnest until the turn of the century. The number of homesteads that were taken up in different periods clearly illustrates this. It is common knowledge that the Canadian government grants every settler a homestead of 160 acres (or 64 hectares), a so-called "quarter-section." The settler must be or must become a British subject; he must pay a fee of $10, and he must live on and cultivate the land for three years before it becomes his property. In most of the districts the settler may, under similar conditions, pick up the option for an additional quarter-section of government land at the same time, and for that he has to pay $3.00 per acre at the time of acquisition. He then has received a total of 128 hectares for some 2000 Marks. During the period from 1884 to 1898 the number of homesteads taken up annually varied between 2,000 and 5,000. By 1902, the number had increased to 14,600, and the average from 1903 to 1908 was 34,800.

The fact that the free land in the United States has more or less been divided up is considered to be the strongest reason for the enormous increase in immigration here. Thus settlers wanting to farm in the New World are beginning to turn to the Canadian West. At the same time, a significantly large stream of farmers come from the United States itself. They have sold their property there at a good price, and they take up a free homestead here, or they buy cultivated land. They are able, then, with land prices that are still so much lower here, to own a far bigger farm than would have been possible south of the border. During the past year 59,000 of the immigrants into Canada were from the United States — as compared with 52,000 from Great Britain and only 34,000 from all the other countries combined. In the months of April and May of this year [1909] alone, 23,700 Americans came — 53 percent more than in the same period of 1908. In Canada, the government and the people consider the Americans to be by far the most welcome settlers. In the first place they usually bring along capital, and in the second place they all have experience with farming under similar conditions. In southern Saskatchewan, too, the immigrants from the United States have contributed their fair share, or rather more than their fair share, to the enormous upswing in agriculture. The American farms are, as a rule, considered to be model farms, and what I have seen so far confirms this belief. It must be mentioned, however, that a surprisingly large number of these "Americans" are of German or Scandinavian origin; their wanderlust does not let them rest.

Especially in the area surrounding Regina there are many farmers who have come directly from Germany, and next to the Americans they probably have the best reputation as farmers — and also as individuals. However, they themselves deplore very strongly the fact that everybody who comes from Eastern Europe is called German, not only here but all over western Canada. In the city of Regina there exists a very large "German quarter" that is mainly populated by Galicians who don't even understand German. Of course, we Germans get similar treatment in the United States; in press and literature there, they put the German "Herr" before every Hungarian, Serbian, or Russian name.

Of all the genuine German farms in the Regina area, I would like to talk about a particular one in greater detail because its development and conditions seem to be typical not only of the German farms but indeed of the farms of the area in general.

There could be no doubt whatsoever that Mr. John Zinkhan, despite his formidable name, was a good German. The moment we met in the middle of the Canadian prairie where he was busy haying, we recognized each other as fellow-countrymen by our mutual Frankfurt dialect. Mr. Zinkhan was a stone-mason, probably called Hannes at the time when, in the Eighties, he left behind the apple-cider and headed for the newest western frontier whose attractions were then being broadcast loudly all over Europe by the CPR. But there was no work for a stone-mason in the new country where everybody made do with tents, shacks, and, in isolated cases at best, some brick buildings. So, the young man from Frankfurt who had come over with nothing but his two strong arms to rely on, worked as a bricklayer. Like all the other workers in this country he had only one goal: to put away enough money to acquire some oxen and the most essential farm implements. After a few years he had accomplished that and took up a homestead; not much later he picked up an option for an additional quarter-section of government land. At the start, the young farmer had to work hard and had barely enough to eat. There was drought and frost, frost and drought; and the yields remained poor year after year. A little earlier I talked about the time when the hopes for western Canada's rich soil appeared to be gone for good. Only the hardiest of the pioneers persevered,

The original Zinkhan home

Courtesy of Mr. & Mrs. Herman Zinkhan

and Zinkhan was one of them. Besides, it could be that a bricklayer, even though he comes from Frankfurt, does not turn into a skilled farmer immediately. However, many go through this experience here. Nobody sits securely in the saddle; and necessity teaches one to pray and to work the soil.

Nobody whom he nowadays shows across his fields will doubt that the bricklayer from Frankfurt has indeed become a farmer. Five quarter-sections (i.e., 320 hectares) he calls his own. Of all this, the government gave him 64 hectares for $480. Today both farms lie idle and are only leased out for hay, because they lie a day's journey away from the owner's present residence. In 1898 he bought a quarter-section close to Regina for the minimal sum of $3.00 per acre and, in 1900, two adjoining quarter-sections for $11 per acre — still cheap enough. Of these three quarter-sections, two are presently under cultivation: about 160 acres in wheat, 80 acres in oats, and 80 acres in summer fallow. His method of land cultivation is already quite advanced for Saskatchewan. It is a three-field system which, as a rule, works as follows: in the first year, the wheat is seeded after thorough ploughing; in the second year, the stubble is burnt down and, without ploughing, the wheat is sown; and in the third year, the field lies fallow. This year a small portion has been damaged by hail, but all in all the crop looks as healthy and full as one could wish. The work is done by the farmer himself. Only the two oldest, a boy of 14 and a daughter of 15, help. Even at harvest time a man is hired only when time runs short. Twelve horses and eighteen head of cattle round out the property; and the solid stone building, a rarity in this part of the country, points to the owner's former trade. The hot-air heating system, however, which means a great saving in these extreme winter temperatures, is quite common even in the rural community.

Now, what is really the value of a farm like this one of Zinkhan's in western Canada? Twelve dollars per acre has been offered for the homestead, which is a distance of ten miles from the next railway stop, and $20 per acre for the government land picked up through option—because it is only one mile away from the railway station. The land of the main farm not under cultivation can be estimated at the same price; but since it is located only five miles out of Regina, it probably will bring more. The cultivated land, to judge by the money paid for neighbouring farms, can be valued at $35 per acre. All this would add up to $20,000. All things considered, then, one can indeed say that the man who, 25 years ago, started out without a penny, is today worth some 100,000 Marks. This he earned with no extra income — solely from working his fields. This latter point is the most remarkable one and is characteristic for western Canada. For by no means have we chosen an exceptional case. Nearly half of the farmers started out the way Zinkhan did, and many, though not all, have had similar success. Not all of them — especially among the Germans, and this is a common complaint — take as much interest in matters that lie beyond the confines of their own fields. Mr. Zinkhan, however, has been a member of the School

Board for years, and he can sing a tune about school attendance of the different nationalities which is quite a departure from "Deutschland, Deutschland über alles." Next winter he himself is going to send his daughter to the College of Agriculture — and his son a year later. The daughter will be taking a six-months' course in home economics. What, after all, is more important for the success of a farm than an efficient housewife?

That one can become a good housewife through experience as well was convincingly demonstrated to us by the "Missus" who served us a hefty evening meal. Only one thing was missing, the "Stoffche" [Frankfurt apple cider]. Without it how were we to drink to the city on the old Main River here in this northern prairie? But this is the great drawback of Saskatchewan: it produces neither apples nor apple-wine. . . .

The main-line of the CPR leads from Regina westward going some 500 kilometres through an area which, up to now, because of its dryness, has been looked upon as a desolate prairie land forever unfit for cultivation and only partly suitable for large-scale ranching and cattle breeding. Originally the CPR was supposed to run from Winnipeg northwest to Edmonton and was to cross the Rocky Mountains at the Yellow Head Pass. The Canadian government, however, insisted upon as direct a line as possible between the Atlantic coast and the Pacific naval port of Esquimalt; therefore the present route, which for two decades has borne the stigma of an economic monstrosity, was chosen for political and military reasons. Lately, it seems to have been gradually recognized that even this land is not as bad as it had appeared to be. In general, the soil is considered very usable, and it is hoped that the desert can be transformed into good farmland through the application of a dry-farming system. This system merely attempts to compensate for the lack of precipitation by applying a suitable method of soil cultivation — or, to be more specific, by carefully retaining and utilizing every drop of moisture. In the most arid districts of Nebraska and other states, this method is said to be surprisingly successful. Here in Canada it will of course be applied on a large scale only when the better land has been allotted and the land-hungry settlers finally turn to the barren prairie of western Saskatchewan. So far, however, while travelling through this part of the country one sees for a whole day at a stretch not much more than dry prairie. More than nine-tenths of the visitors to Canada use this main-line of the CPR, and their general impression of the agricultural achievements and prospects of the Northwest is therefore considerably less favourable than the country actually deserves.

To me personally it seemed more interesting and of greater benefit to skirt the barren land and to see more of those parts of Canada which are already under cultivation, or are expected to become farmland in the near future. From Regina a line runs north to Prince Albert. This line was originally independent, later belonged to the CPR system, and today is a part of the Canadian Northern Railway. This railway is already 18 years old, but for a whole decade the prairie on both sides of its tracks lay unused and unwanted. Only the land between Saskatoon and Prince Albert along the northern third of the route has been settled since the mid-Nineties. A leading official of the CPR, who happens to be on the train, explains to me that the reason for this earlier neglect of the whole southern area can be attributed to accidental and unfounded prejudices of the first settlers of western Canada. If they were indeed only prejudices, they must have been very strong ones to drive thousands of immigrants to the North Saskatchewan River and to the Battle River, where people often had to walk hundreds of miles before they heard the whistle of a locomotive, when right here, to the left and to the right of the railway line, there was plenty of free land available. It is true that here and there the land is cut-up and rolling, but this is the only real disadvantage I could discover. The soil itself is considered excellent by residents and visitors alike. Beyond Regina one sees magnificent wheat and oat fields, and very beautiful flax; barley also seems to do well. After that, low bush-country again. Much open prairie, whose brownish-green grass cover seems to extend endlessly until somewhere in the distance a black ploughed field appears; beyond that, frequently a yellow wheat field and, beside it, a wide area of green oats. In most cases, the farmers still live in quite humble wooden houses, more often in even smaller cabins called shacks — four walls made of boards or tar-paper put on the bare floor, and an equally primitive roof on top of it. From all this, one can easily see that this stretch was settled much more recently than the area along the Winnipeg-Regina main-line.

"Here you can see what it looked like further to the east where we lived fifteen, even ten years ago." So lectures an old farmer from Manitoba who sat down next to me on the platform-step. "In another ten years, you will find here the same agricultural development, the same beautiful houses and well-to-do farms you drove past on the CPR yesterday or the day before yesterday." He speaks in an impressive literary style — the good old man — and a theological tract in the pocket of his jacket reveals where he picked it up. But his calloused hands prove that he not only talks about the agricultural development, but has also helped to shape it. It is always the same story: fifteen years ago, he came as a penniless worker from eastern Canada, started to farm here, and sold out this spring. That these fifteen years were not spent in vain is confirmed by the sweeping gesture of his hand and by his laughter, which is almost broader and more convincing than the heavy golden watch chain dangling from his pocket. Now he is on his way to visit his son who, three years ago, took up a homestead here, bought more land in the meantime, and is very satisfied with the yield. By the way, here — unlike on the CPR mainline — there are still enough homesteads available. I met a young German merchant who had just taken one up. It is not at all far from the rail line and, in the opinion of his relatives who live close by, it is excellent land.

III AROUND ROSTHERN

Calgary (Alberta) in August

The City of Saskatoon is about to become for central and northern Saskatchewan what Regina has already been for a long time in the south of the province. Seven years ago it had a population of 250 inhabitants; today, according to the most conservative estimates, it numbers 8,000. It is a well-built, snug little city, beautifully framed by the South Saskatchewan River. It also has its Sachsenhausen [suburb of Frankfurt] called Nutana, which looks down on Saskatoon not only because of its higher elevation and more beautiful view, but also because it is the future site of the new University of Saskatchewan. There have been bitter fights between Regina and Saskatoon about this university, for the two cities are forever feuding and contending jealously for precedence on every occasion like the queens of the old saga. Today, Regina is still ahead: larger, more beautiful, and of greater economic importance. After all, it is the older, the seat of government and the centre of the richest wheatland. In the course of time, however, it may well be overtaken by Saskatoon — primarily because, later on, three transcontinental lines will pass through that city. That is the route which originally was planned by the CPR. Three years ago the Canadian Northern opened this stretch of its Winnipeg-Edmonton main-line, and will continue through to the Pacific Ocean in the next few years. The new Grand Trunk Pacific Railway also skirts Saskatoon; it is already completed as far as Edmonton, although not yet in operation, and it is scheduled to reach the Pacific Coast near Prince Rupert in 1915. The CPR, too, needs only a few small junction-lines to complete the Winnipeg-Saskatoon-Edmonton run as planned. These will be completed shortly, and it is expected that the CPR also intends to continue on from Edmonton to the coast. Moreover, the country around Saskatoon is less developed but scarcely poorer than that near Regina and at any rate much vaster. Even now the most thriving settlements are expanding west, east, and north as far as Prince Albert. Beyond Prince Albert begin the huge forests, whose far side touches the Arctic Circle. Iron and silver will undoubtedly be found there and other metals and coal as well, so they claim. And once the prairie land has been divided up, it will be worthwhile to clear the forests, and agriculture can then be extended a good distance farther north.

The land between Saskatoon and Prince Albert has been settled by people of all nationalities — Germans, French, Galicians, Russians, Hungarians, and English-Canadians. One hour's drive out of Saskatoon, the prairie gives way to beautiful wheat fields which are kept cleaner than is usually the case. In between these, broad fields of oats and some barley. But here and there sits an honest-to-goodness German farm in the midst of the cultivated land. Clean dwellings, strong sturdy stables, behind them a tidy big manure pile (this is the characteristic feature of the German farm), a large well-kept vegetable garden near the house, bordered with friendly flowers, and dense clusters of trees to the west and the north as windbreaks. Over a wide area, 40 square kilometres or so, there are Germans from southern Russia, mostly Mennonites, but Lutherans and Catholics as well. Rosthern, a town of 1,200 inhabitants — probably more than half of them Germans — forms the centre of the district. In Ontario and Pennsylvania there have been large colonies of German and Russian-German Mennonites for a long time. From there, many thousands of them went to southern Manitoba where they became prosperous, often rich. Around the mid-Nineties and again in the middle of the present decade German Mennonites came into the Rosthern area, partly from there and partly from Russia. In general they have attained great prosperity and this, it would seem, more through hard work and thrift than through advanced farming methods. Outsiders often deplore the primitive farming system of the older Mennonites, and many examples of this can still be seen today. However, the younger generation appears to be progressive and to have more appreciation of modern agriculture and education in general.

Strolling through the streets of Rosthern one notices few English firm names. On the other hand, the British flag is evident in every store window, which leaves no doubt as to the present nationality of the owner. But right beside it a huge sign on a wooden fence announces: "Alpenkräuter [Alpine Herbs], price $1.00 per bottle." Through all the wanderings, thirst has remained typically German! But not just thirst, as is evidenced by the schoolhouse presently under construction, and destined to train Germans as teachers.

It seems to me that this school, although still in its early stages, merits attention beyond its narrow confines — in Germany, and even more in the U.S.A. Not long ago, several professors at the University of Wisconsin complained to me that occasionally among their students, there are graduates of German-American schools who have a good general education, as a rule, but have learned so little English that they can scarcely follow the lectures. A German merchant, theoretically a supporter of those schools, confessed to me that he had had experience with two of their graduates who were unable to compose an English letter. The Germans of the Rosthern area, who are certainly not all Mennonites, want to avoid shortcomings of this kind. They realize that their children must become Canadians, and therefore they want to send them to the public (English) schools. At the same time they do want to retain the German language, not instead of English but in addition to it! The Canadian government permits a foreign language to be taught in the elementary schools if the school district so wishes. Of course, all German communities in the area take advantage of this, but it is extremely difficult for them to find teachers qualified to teach German. It is the purpose of the new school to help remedy this situation and to train young men and women, non-Germans as well, if they apply, to become teachers, English-Canadian teachers qualified to teach German. Even though the teaching of the German language may go hand in

Where Wheat is King

Canadian Pacific Railway Lands

Why not own a Farm in

Saskatchewan

THE AGRICULTURAL PROVINCE

Rich Land along new lines of Railway

At $10.00 To $20.00 per Acre

Are you farming for pleasure or profit? If for profit, consider this: Saskatchewan soil is capable of raising from twenty to forty bushels of wheat per acre. Saskatchewan grew last year 90,215,000 bushels of wheat; 105,465,000 bushels of oats; 7,833,000 bushels of barley, and 4,448,700 bushels of flax; and yet the land cultivated was only one-twentieth of the area of the province. There are millions of acres still available for settlers. These lands yield banner crops of wheat, oats and all small grains, and they cannot be surpassed for mixed farming and dairying. Conveniently located markets at points

ALONG THE LINES OF THE CANADIAN PACIFIC RAILWAY

assist the farmers to dispose of their produce at the highest prices.

You can sell your higher-priced land and buy outright a larger tract of the choicest land in Saskatchewan ideally located, pay all your moving expenses, and have enough money left to build your house and barns and fence your own new farm. Or if you are now a **renter**, you can pay down from $200 to $300 for a choice quarter section along the new lines of the Canadian Pacific Railway, and the balance out of the crops.

For instance, on a 160 acre farm at $10 an acre you would make a cash payment of only $239.70; then there would be only the interest, $81.62 at the end of the first year, and after that nine annual instalments of $200. Both the man with considerable money and the man with only a small bank account will find opportunity, health and happiness here. Good neighbors, easy access to markets, excellent schools and churches.

Saskatchewan is the Centre of the West

And this is your opportunity to join in making it

The Wheat Centre of the World

Canadian Pacific Railway Land Dept., Winnipeg, Manitoba

F. T. GRIFFIN, Land Commissioner   J. L. DOUPE, Asst. Land Commissioner

Courtesy of Saskatchewan Archives

From the Heart of the Saskatchewan Valley (Winnipeg, 1910)

hand with the fostering of German culture and civilization, this need not detract from the main objective or from Canadianism. The graduates, of course, will have to pass the regular state examination for teachers. They will then be employed in the schools of German communities and teach the regular subjects in English, plus one or one and one-half hours of German per day. This Teachers' College of Rosthern deserves the interest and support of the Germans in the homeland. It seems to me a good example for German settlements in countries of comparable culture.

Coming from the south and looking out of the left train window at the station of Rosthern, the traveller sees a clean and prosperous town which is, in the final analysis, hardly different from the others. "But what if he looks out the right coach window!" the barber, a member of the municipal Council, exclaims with a shudder. He is from Berlin and has not lost the sense of beauty and order which that city is known for. To the right side of the track, you see, the traveller would discover a dozen straw-thatched roofs scarcely above ground, and the affluent citizens fear that the traveller might draw the conclusion, from these sod huts, that there were also less well-to-do people in this town. The fear is entirely unfounded, for nothing can give a stranger a better idea of this country's potential than visiting these sod huts and listening to the stories of the occupants.

Several years ago newly immigrated Hungarians came to Rosthern and found no place to stay. Because winter, with temperatures down to −45°C, was approaching, they had the clever idea of digging themselves into the ground to a depth of 1½ metres with only a small window under the roof looking out above ground level. In other towns of western Canada, a large number of immigrants without means live for the most part in tents or in the flimsy shacks mentioned before. But the sod huts are really much more practical. They can be fixed up quite comfortably: first down three steps, into a small entrance room with a stove; then down still lower there is a large room where the "better" folks put in a deal floor. People point out that a family hardly ever lives here longer than a year; then they move up, and that not only in lodging. Over there, a sturdy middle-aged woman is sitting at the door of her house and knitting a good woollen stocking. She tells me that she is a Catholic German, that she came from Bessarabia a year ago together with her husband and four grown sons, and that the expensive trip ate up so much money that they ran into debt. The men went to work as labourers, and within the year they earned more than enough to pay it off. Now they are in North Battleford, and each one has taken up a homestead, five adjoining quarter-sections. The family therefore owns a farm of 320 hectares, and the land up there is known to be excellent. They will get equipment and cattle on the instalment plan and the government will advance seed, if necessary. If the men are as efficient as the mother in her spic-and-span sod hut appears to be, then, in a few years' time, there will be another well-to-do family, or more likely, five more well-to-do families.

Whoever thinks this prediction too optimistic should have come with me eight kilometres to the south. Here lives Otto Marquardt of Bromheim, who went to Wolhynia as a young man and came to Canada from there in 1892. He arrived in Winnipeg with $60, worked there for 1½ years and then homesteaded near Rosthern. (He, by the way, is not a Mennonite but a Lutheran.) After paying for a few head of cattle and farming implements, he had a fortune of just $1.00 left. Today, after 15 years, Marquardt has no debts but a considerable bank account and, in addition, three whole sections of land (768 hectares), the sales value of which is estimated at 200,000 Marks by himself and by others who are knowledgeable. His brother, who settled here at the same time and who lives nearby, is said to be just as well off. Marquardt, who is helped by his three sons and one farmhand (during harvest time there are three), has only part of his farmland under cultivation, as is customary. This year there are only about 512 acres of wheat (320 of which are in one single field), 160 acres of oats, and 21 acres of barley. He doesn't want to have anything to do with crop rotation or summer fallow. The soil, he claims, is still too rich for it. For eight consecutive years the same field has produced wheat and the yields have not decreased.

Without any doubt, Marquardt is one of the most successful farmers in the area, but he is in no way an exception. There is a Mr. Heinrich Wider, who, in answer to my question, vigorously denies stemming from East-Prussia. He came from Russia, he says. But then he repeats one more astonished "Astpreiszen" [with a typical East-Prussian accent] so that there is not much doubt in my mind as to his native country. East- and West-Prussia, by the way, seem to be the original homeland of most of the Russian-German Mennonites who live here. Wider only came in 1894 and he started out with a debt of $35. Today his farm comprises 200 hectares and is debt-free. I could tell you of many similar success stories. Of course, there are other less successful ones. An old Russian-German says: "My homestead was sufficient for me. I could always eat my fill — I never had it so good in the old country." Apparently there are very few real failures.

IV A DOUKHOBOR VILLAGE

Calgary (Alberta) in August

The German settlement around Rosthern lies nestled between the North and South Saskatchewan Rivers which here flow nearly parallel in a north-north easterly direction. On the other side of the North Saskatchewan lies a Doukhobor colony of ten villages. Everybody probably still remembers how this Russian sect fought with their government because they refused to do military service. Finally they declared that they would no longer recognize the Tsar's rule because of his injustice. American Quakers and Count Tolstoi helped them emigrate to Canada, and the majority of them today live at the eastern border of the Province of Saskatchewan, in the area around Yorkton. While at Rosthern I took the opportunity of visiting at least their branch colony. The village nearest to it, Petrowka [Petrofka?], is situated about 59 kilometres to the west. The road runs right through the German district: first, prairie alternating with well-cultivated fields, gradually changing into low bush country, then clusters of trees, a sparse copse, and we finally reach the river passing through a real forest. It meanders among the wooded hills like a shining ribbon in the August midday sun. Only straight across is the hilltop cleared; broad yellow wheatfields beckon, and in front of them there lies an honest-to-goodness straw-thatched peasant village. The name of the ferryman who takes us across is Nicholas Postnikoff, and his English vocabulary consists of the words "ten cents." We drive up the hill and now, here in the middle of Canada, the land of detached farms, we are faced with the strange sight of an authentic small Russian village: low, elongated one-storey houses, with the narrow sides facing the village road, the front third being the living quarters, the rest stables; the roof made of dirt and straw, the window frames painted with blue and red designs. Beside the house and exactly of the same height, the hay is stacked in such a way that the yard is completely and evenly enclosed on three sides. The most noticeable interior features of the one house that I saw were a huge stove, a few foreign-looking earthenware bowls, and considerable dirt. On the whole, this village looked poor and ill-kept, something totally unexpected in this country. Most of the men were out in the fields, and of the people remaining in the village, only one person understood a little bit of English, so that even he could provide me with only very little information.

The most interesting information about the Doukhobors, I owe to a German who lives nearby. It was confirmed and added to by private parties as well as by government officials in Rosthern and Saskatoon. This German farmer, Herman Fast, a Mennonite from southern Russia, had originally been a teacher by profession and had lived many years in the Crimea. Later on, in Constanza, he ran a school for children orphaned by the Armenian atrocities; eight years ago he came to Canada with his family and settled in the vicinity of Rosthern as a farmer. In this time he has had to return to the classroom twice. Three years ago, when the people of Rosthern started out modestly with their Teachers' College, he was the first to teach there. But after a year he took up residence on the west side of the Saskatchewan River, helped the Doukhobors to found their first school and ran it, as its principal, until last year. Up to then, schools were absolutely anathema to the Doukhobors; in the other villages, especially in the main colony near Yorkton, there are no schools to this day.

This branch colony is already strongly emancipated in many other respects as well. Much as that is a blessing for their inhabitants, it was a disappointment to me that I was no longer able to see it in its original state. By that I don't mean so much their original state of nudity as their communist system of economy. Even today the colonies in the Yorkton district are subject to epidemic attacks of religious mania. On a lovely Sunday morning only a couple of weeks ago, one village shocked the Canadian farmers on their way to church when some of its inhabitants marched nude into the prairie. In their midst they had a cart bearing the corpse of an old woman, also nude and uncovered, which they simply threw on the grass-covered prairie and left to the beasts of heaven and earth. Canadian farmers later buried the corpse. I would not have believed or reported this story had it not been officially confirmed.

The Doukhobors of the Yorkton district still practise a strict form of communism. Their leader, Peter Veregin [*sic*], rules with absolute authority. For some time now, he has declared not only the schools but also any form of divine service to be illicit and sinful. They worship the man himself as the resurrected Son of God. The material consequences of this worship are high contributions, regular as well as special, which Veregin collects from the individual, economically independent communities. The contributions are supposed to be used for the benefit of the whole sect. But all my sources agree that Veregin bleeds his fellow countrymen white solely for his personal gain. Outside of his own community he is unanimously described as a domineering, shrewd and unscrupulous cheat. Economically, he has the sect well organized. They are well equipped with agricultural machines and, because they are sitting on excellent land, their returns must be considerable. The people themselves, however, are said to show little interest in work and have no mind for technical progress. The consensus is that the majority still live as miserably as before.

The branch colony on the North Saskatchewan River now maintains only loose ties with the entire colony. Above all they have private property, and the weaker Veregin's influence became, the better the agricultural operation grew. The fields that I saw myself were indeed cleanly kept, and the reason that the crop was not doing quite as well as in other areas might be due to the sandier soil. In Petrowka, the divine service has been reintroduced, probably under the influence of the Mennonites. Also the founding of the school there is obviously Mr. Fast's doing. Years ago, an American Quaker lady bequeathed $60,000 for Doukhobor schools, but

Veregin vetoed the bequest. The Petrowka schoolhouse, partly built with this money, is an unusually nice little building which would be a credit to any German rural community. The language of instruction is English, but Russian has been proposed as a second language. The children are described as intelligent and very eager to learn, and the newly awakened interest of the parents is so strong that children from several villages in the branch colony are being sent to school in Petrowka — even though they have to stay in town throughout the winter, partly because of the distance home and partly because of the cold.

Here in the far West, it is taken for granted that the traveller finds the utmost hospitality at every farmhouse. For a special reason, however, I must mention the tremendous reception at the Fast farm. There we had fresh ears of corn, small but succulent, grown on the farm this year for the first time. In Germany, as you know, this excellent vegetable is not known as human food except to boys who are in the habit of pilfering it from the field — assuming that boys have not changed for the better since our days. In the U.S., however, one is often served corn-on-the-cob with one's meals for weeks on end. Originally, corn was a crop of the hot midwestern States; and as a primary crop, it is that to this day. For years it has pushed farther north, but it came as a surprise to me that it had reached Canada, this land of short summers — and not only the warm southern Alberta but also the far Northwest. It is probably safe to assume that it won't become a regular crop up here. In any case, it is a great experience when right before my eyes, outside on the prairie, the sky that has ripened the corn I have just eaten presents the magnificent spectacle of the Northern Lights. This phenomenon can be seen here every evening. Between 9:00 and 9:30, long after the land has sunk into deep darkness, a wide, long, horizontal strip on the northern sky slowly brightens to a milky-white glow. In an ever-increasing movement, to the left then to the right, in different places, the pale, almost luminously pale cones of light rise up, descend, rise again and disappear. The wide band grows weak, now here, now there, and then grows stronger again. Suddenly, a rocket — a whole sheaf of milky-white light — shoots up and slowly collapses. Whole volcanoes cast up an opalescent glow. And above us the stars shine peacefully.

* * *

Long after the Northern Lights have disappeared, the eyes and the mind hold them fast. But just as the horse, smelling home, returns at a faster trot over the prairie sod, I must return once more in my thoughts to those corncobs, and to how the will and the spirit of Man has wakened this prairie to life and work and production in the land of the Northern Lights. Indeed, nothing is more marvellous on this earth than man!

V EDMONTON

Calgary (Alberta) in August

For the most part, the main-line of the Canadian Northern Railway from Saskatoon to Edmonton cuts through the land between the North Saskatchewan River and the Battle River to the south of it. Here there is a soil that has long been reputed the best and that drew settlers up here long before the railway came. Unfortunately, the only train on the line crosses through this district during the night; so anyone passing through here must accept the praise of the region strictly from hearsay. The first quarter of the stretch, which is crossed while there is still daylight, is through obviously newly settled country. The railway was completed only a few years ago, and the villages we get to see here are still in their infancy. What we call a village, of course, does not exist in Canada, except for Doukhobor settlements, because each farmer lives on his own land, as is customary under the single-farm system. From its very beginning, then, even the smallest hick-town considers itself a city, and it is indeed quite modest if it does not think of itself immediately as a future metropolis. There was a little hamlet X where I counted exactly eight little wooden houses. The railway station, being number nine, completed the town. On the other side of the tracks, however, a large sign had been erected which literally shouted to the traveller: "Stay in X! Why go further? You can do better business here than anywhere else! — THE BOARD OF TRADE."

Most towns try to present their seven wonders right away — on a silver platter — to the traveller who gets to know them only through the train window. The main business street, with only one row of buildings facing the railroad tracks, usually lies right behind the station. As a rule the houses are built of wood. Only in bigger towns are there also some brick buildings in between. The hotel is probably the most solid construction; it also flashes its name the farthest out into the world. Besides the hotel there are, depending on the size of the place, one or two shacks, or sometimes even actual warehouses with agricultural implements. The American Harvester Trust and the Canadian Massey-Harris Co. are represented in almost every one-horse town. The spread of Canadian banks is surprising. In a place like Rosthern, three or four of them have branch offices, and even at the smallest station the passer-by is greeted by the proud name of one of the large banks among the dozen little wooden houses. Then beside the bank is a good-sized store where the farmer and his wife can get all their supplies, from canned vegetables to a raincoat, fashion-wares, cutlery, and hosiery. Moreover, a man can sell his land here or add to it because the general merchant is most certainly also involved in land speculation, although a real estate man has probably put up his shack right beside him. Finally, a livery stable, with fodder sales and horsetrading as a sideline, must be mentioned here. Yet the most striking thing at every station is,

Courtesy of Saskatchewan Archives

Elevators at Rosthern

without exception, a huge elevator for cleaning and storing grain; often there are two or three — up to twelve — of these, and one gauges the prosperity of the area by their number. Rosthern, for instance, has ten. The entire town which belongs to such an impressive "railway street" may number perhaps not more than two hundred people, but it satisfies the needs of a large and well-to-do farm district.

The towns, even the larger ones, differ from those already described more in size than in type. They have, after all, the same economic character as the collection and distribution centres of an agricultural district. The size and prosperity of this area correspond to the size and prosperity of the town. According to this principle, Edmonton undoubtedly has an important future in the Province of Alberta. Just as Calgary is the focal point in the south, so Edmonton is that in central Alberta, and between these two cities exactly the same kind of rivalry prevails as in Saskatchewan between Saskatoon and Regina. Like Regina, Calgary is the older and, to this date, bigger city because it was built following the construction of the CPR. But like Saskatoon, in a few years Edmonton will be the junction of two or maybe three transcontinental lines — the Grand Trunk Pacific, the Canadian Northern, and the CPR. The area surrounding Calgary is perhaps somewhat richer than that around Edmonton, but it has less potential for expansion. Down here the Rocky Mountains come close to Calgary while in central Alberta they curve outward sharply, and at least part of the area around Edmonton is suitable for agriculture. Above all, Edmonton dominates the whole North-country which only a short time ago was considered a useless semi-arctic region. Meanwhile, it has been noted—and, wherever tested, confirmed — that a large part (possibly the largest) of this area is highly suitable for agriculture.

As early as 1893 grain grown near Peace River landing, 400 kilometres northwest of Edmonton, received the first prize at the Chicago World Exhibition. At that time this was probably considered only a freak happening, and, in any case, no more attention was paid to it. In the meantime, a rather strong settlement has formed there which is successfully growing wheat. But if you go down (i.e., northward) on the Peace River another 500 kilometres, you come, near Fort Vermillion, to another colony of farmers, of whom one alone grew about 260 acres of wheat during the last year. We most likely all have the preconceived notion that it must be colder in the north than in the south, and in Canada one further assumes that the temperature gets colder toward the west. The first is partly erroneous, the latter totally. All of Alberta is considerably warmer than Saskatchewan, its neighbour to the east; and the northern parts do indeed have colder winters than the southern ones most of the time, but they also have hotter summers. Fort Vermillion, situated 600 kilometres north of Edmonton, at 58°27′ North latitude, naturally has a cold winter, which lasts from October to April inclusive. But the heat of the five summer months is strong enough to bring the crops to maturity in time. In June of last year, Fort Vermillion reached the highest temperature in all of Alberta, 31.8°C, and even in May it was nearly that hot. Of course, there was frost in September — but at that time frost also occurs in the south — and the minimum temperature for the month was only 2.5°C lower than that of Cardston in the extreme south of Alberta. Therefore there is no question at all that even this extreme northern area is technically suitable for agriculture. It will become economically feasible as well on the day when the railway reaches here, and this day is no longer far off. The Grand Trunk Pacific already has decided to lay track from Edmonton to the Peace River area. The Canadian Northern, indeed, has already penetrated a good distance into the north, and in the course of the next year they hope to reach Athabasca Landing, where a large fertile area is waiting to be opened up. From there as well as from the southern Peace River region, they can later push ahead to Fort Vermillion, although this is still a considerable distance.

The City of Edmonton was originally a fur-trading post of the Hudson's Bay Company. Then, at the end of the mid-Seventies, when the CPR was considering this northern line to the Pacific, the first of the bold, speculating settlers came driving up here from Winnipeg in their ox-carts. One can imagine their disappointment when the line was finally built 300 kilometres to the south, and neither they nor their descendants have forgiven the CPR for that to this day. Yet the hardy pioneers persevered although the settlement, the northernmost in the country, did not make any progress for decades. To appease them, the CPR constructed a branch-line up from Calgary. The land along the tracks developed exceedingly well, but Edmonton made only slow progress. Only the new century brought a change. This was partly attributable to the general economic upswing, but much more to the announcement of — and most of all to the completion of — a direct northern rail line up from Winnipeg. Seven years ago the city had a population of 3,000; today it has 24,000. I have found no city which has made its development so much its business as Edmonton. With some exaggeration one could indeed say that the whole population talks about nothing else, works for nothing else, lives for nothing else. Of these statements, the first can be taken quite literally.

It is impossible to sit in a hotel lobby for five minutes without a friendly gentleman sitting down in the chair to your left, puffing away on his short pipe, spitting past you into the spittoon on your right and remarking that the weather is indeed beautiful . . . But it is like that in Edmonton throughout the year . . . No better place to live! . . . And the way the country is developing — after a few years every farmer a half-millionaire! . . . Everybody comes to Edmonton to buy supplies or to conclude some other business . . . No better place in all of Canada for a business man or a manufacturer to settle down! . . . Do you know at all how this city is growing? . . . (Then follow the figures given above with varying additions to the present population figures . . .) But that is nothing for a city in such a location! . . . One day the Chicago of the North will be located here! You can bet your life on that! . . . Now tell me, wouldn't you be interested in a piece of property? . . . Today you can still have it for

$2,000 and in two years it will be worth ten times that much . . . etc., etc. . . . (Conversation to be continued by any real estate man.)

A country in the process of being settled is, of course, overrun by real estate agents and land speculators. In the Canadian West more or less everybody speculates in land. When you ask in the various places how people have made their fortune, you learn with surprising regularity that the medium-sized fortunes have been acquired by cultivating the soil, the very big ones through speculation and trading of land. Even in the case of substantial merchants and manufacturers, as far as they exist, people usually say that they became rich because of their knack with real estate, either urban or rural. All prosperity comes from the land in this new country. At least one interesting parallel to [Werner] Sombart's theory of the origin of great fortunes! Thus it is not surprising that the buying and selling of real estate is the main topic of conversation everywhere. Friendly offers, such as the one just described, are sometimes put to strangers in hotels in other towns as well. But nowhere, it seems, does land speculation so dominate people's minds as in Edmonton. It takes a hard-headed person indeed to escape from this city without being immortalized in their land register. Even a lack of funds is not sufficient protection because paying by instalments is the usual method of land purchasing. The people have already had one bad experience with their over-optimistic speculating in local patriotism, for Edmonton appears to be the only city in western Canada which was seriously affected by the recession of 1907, and it would seem that it still has not quite recovered from it economically. And yet, speculation is again leaping merrily ahead.

There is no question, however, that Edmonton is going to have a great future. There is also no question that its citizens not only gamble on this prospect, but indeed make every effort to make it a reality. One would do them an injustice if one considered personal monetary gain to be the sole motive for their lasting enthusiasm and propaganda for the development of Edmonton. However, the future of these western Canadian cities quite simply depends less on their citizens than on the number and the prosperity of the farmers who drive in to trade with them. But perhaps Edmonton in particular has the prospect of growing beyond being an exclusively agricultural city, for it has coal. The local enthusiasts dream of developing heavy industry, and even now they can be proud of an impressive number of mines situated within a tight semi-circle around the city. For the time being, however, these mines are of limited capacity. If I am not mistaken, the largest employs thirty miners, others only one or two. Undoubtedly there are an extraordinary number of coal seams which are still untouched, but the richness of their deposits and their workability have, so it seems, not yet been sufficiently examined. That Edmonton itself is sitting on coal can be taken quite literally; besides, this might also explain the nervous mobility of its population. [Here the writer is thinking of the German idiom *wie auf Kohlen sitzen,* "like sitting on (hot) coals."]

The North Saskatchewan River embraces the city in a sharp curve, and as it has dug itself down into the plateau about 100 metres, Edmonton enjoys an unusually beautiful location in this otherwise flat prairie land. One part of the elevation across the river is still overgrown with trees, and another part bears the stately suburb of Strathcona, end of the line for the CPR and seat of the provincial university. Edmonton itself is the seat of the provincial government for which, at the present time, a Parliament Building is being erected which will satisfy the most ambitious aspirations. The buildings housing the branches of the big banks are equally impressive and, what is more, tasteful. The Edmontonians, however, like the Winnipeggers, pride themselves on nothing so much as on the width of their streets. In that respect they could equal the people of Frankfurt in driving four-in-hand carriages on each side of the street, even with all four horses abreast. But for the time being they prefer the street cars because these still have the appeal of novelty, and the conductors are instructed to tell every stranger that this was the first tramline west of Winnipeg. For they beat the rival city of Calgary to it by just a few weeks — sweet revenge for the fact that Calgary had beaten them with the transcontinental line by thirty years.

I personally found the tram more conspicuous by its absence than by its presence; especially on Sunday, when it "rests" — as one official explained it — partly for fear of God and partly for fear of the powerhouse, which has to be overhauled once a week.

VI AMERICAN AND ENGLISH IMMIGRANTS

Calgary (Alberta) in August

The rural district around Edmonton — and I refer to a very large area — is much praised for its fertility. It was originally, and is partly to this day, covered with low forest and bush, a fact that makes the initial cultivation quite difficult and expensive, but pays off doubly in yield later on because of the greater and longer-lasting richness of the forest soil as compared to that of the prairie soil. I visited the so-called Clover Bar district, stretching to the east of the city, which thoroughly confirms the good things one hears of the area. In contrast to Saskatchewan, whose agriculture relies mainly on wheat, almost the entire Province of Alberta goes in for predominantly mixed farming. This is to some degree due to the difference in climate; moreover, Alberta generally was settled a little earlier, and its agriculture as a whole is technically more advanced. The fields I saw — mostly oats, then barley and to a lesser degree wheat — showed considerable hail damage in patches, but apart from that the crops were unmistakably fuller and better than in the parts of Saskatchewan that I had visited, although they were obviously not tended as carefully as is the rule especially in the German districts of Canada. This remark, however, does not apply to the farm of one American about which I would like to report briefly.

Mr. Warner's farm differs from those of his neighbours at first glance in that the house is sitting neither up front near the road nor amidst the fields visible from afar. We open the barbed wire fence, which, in Canada as well as in the U.S., surrounds all farm property, and drive now more than one kilometre, between the most magnificent oat field of a good 134 acres to the left and a somewhat smaller wheat field to the right where the cutting is nearly completed. Then we continue on a pretty forest path for some five minutes. After such a beautiful drive, the European would now expect to find at least a lordly manor. But as the woods open up, what do we see? On one side spacious stables of unhewn logs, thickly thatched in the style of the most primitive log huts, on the other side an unusually large vegetable garden; and only at the very last does the eye discover at the rear edge of the rather narrow clearing a shack — very small, old, and shabby, but on closer inspection extremely cleanly kept. This is typical of the Canadian farmer: landed property like an aristocratic estate, and capital greater than that of many a knightly gentleman because debt is so far still at a minimum, but the housing, clothing, work, and way of life of a big farmer. Education and culture in this refuge for all nationalities are naturally quite varied; the German national usually seems to be superior to his neighbours in both. Only the farmer from the U.S. is sometimes ahead of him in education and, most frequently, in outward refinement.

This Mr. Warner came up here from Nebraska ten years ago with $6,000 or so and bought himself 800 acres — that is, 320 hectares — for

$6.00 per acre, three-quarters of an hour from Edmonton. The rest of the money just sufficed to buy a few head of cattle and some implements, a little house and stables, primitive but solid enough to last to this day. His aim was to do more intensive farming than would have been possible on a homestead out in the prairies. As I approach, he is working in the vegetable field, and he may indeed show with pride what technically advanced operation and careful work can extract from even this cold country where the thermometer has been known to drop to −50°C. Nearly all vegetables grown in our country — beets, lettuce, and potatoes — can be found here. Even asparagus is not missing; of course I cannot say anything about its quality at this time of the year, though it can hardly be worse than elsewhere in America. From the cornfield, however, very beautiful albeit somewhat small corncobs were brought to the table in the evening. There are long rows of strawberry patches beside the corn, and dozens of kindergarten classes could get upset stomachs with the fruit of the raspberry, currant, and gooseberry bushes here. The forest goes right down to the river bank, but before we get there we find the grazing herd, sixty strapping brown fellows, the most beautiful animals I've seen in Canada so far. Warner has sold 80 hectares of forest near the river to a company of which he himself is a shareholder, in order to set up a recreation park with steamer traffic from Edmonton. Incidentally, up to now the rather limited navigability of the upper Saskatchewan River has hardly been used at all, but in the past, gold was panned on Warner's shore property — though for years that has no longer been worth the trouble. However, it is said that coal can be found in the ground everywhere, even here, and a short time ago the neighbours on both sides of him sold out, the one for $100 and the other for $120 per acre. Even without coal, Warner's farm today would bring seven times the purchasing price of 1899. Of his remaining 240 hectares, about 100 hectares seem to be forest. The rest is under cultivation — this year predominantly oats, less wheat, some barley, and quite a large field of red clover as well as forage crops. Part of the wheat was seeded in the fall and is doing very well; in the future Warner plans to sow only winter wheat, and he says successful experiments have already been carried out with it in the Peace River district. It is not long ago at all that the presumed safe cultivation limit for winter wheat ran far to the south of the U.S. border; but for a few years southern Alberta has been growing the hardiest winter wheat, and now it is already advancing into central Alberta and, experimentally, into Canada's northernmost settled region. A marvellous step forward in Man's conquest of the land!

I was referred to Mr. Warner's farm because all of the American settlers I had met here until then were of German or Scandinavian origin, and because I insisted on meeting a genuine Anglo-American for a change. But, lo and behold, the farmer's efficient wife and his mother both were of Pennsylvanian stock originally from the Palatinate! American immigration is the Alpha and Omega of the Canadian government; the whole country is proud of its appeal for the farmer from "the States" and welcomes him with

From Canada the Grange of the World (Ottawa, 1903)

Courtesy of Saskatchewan Archives

enthusiasm, but whenever one scratches this American immigrant, German blood appears. In this district there also live German nationals and German-speaking Austrians. They have strong and, so I am told, very well-to-do settlements west of Edmonton. Nowhere would a map of nationalities be as colourful as in both the narrower and the broader vicinity of this city. There are eastern Canadians, Germans, Americans, Galicians, Scandinavians, Frenchmen, Scots, and Englishmen.

The least welcome, not only here but in all of western Canada, are the English immigrants. In Edmonton, when I was visiting with a person of responsible position, I happened to meet an employee of the British Colonial Office. Nothwithstanding my presence, the official of the mother-country had to endure a bitter diatribe which, despite the Canadian's veneer of politeness, attested to a long-nursed resentment. They were the same complaints one gets to hear everywhere and from everyone in these parts: that western Canada is regarded as a recreational and correctional institution for those who have become disabled by their struggle for existence in the major cities of England; that these people get used neither to the pioneer farmer's primitive way of life nor to his hard work; that they have never seen a farm in their home country and yet think, with the arrogance of the European city-dweller, they know everything and know everything better; that finally they founder and, because of their personal failure, blacken the reputation of the country. There comes (for instance) such a young city slicker from London in the hope of profiting from the economic boom of the young country without having to work, believing one need only sit on the homestead, which is a gift from the government, and smoke cigarettes until such time as it has become worth a fortune. These complaints are so unanimous that I have heard them even from Englishmen, only they content themselves with making the Londoner the butt of their indignation. However, a closer investigation always reveals that the English *farmers* who came over were at least as successful as others. So the aforementioned British Colonial officer ventured to answer timidly that efforts were already being made to send over farmers whenever possible, whereupon the Canadian indignation easily subsided. It is, however, difficult to see where the English government is supposed to recruit English farmers for emigration; so far they are wisely trying to establish more farmers on their own soil.

Anyone who wanted to gauge the political mood of the Canadians towards their mother-country from the reported complaints about the English settlers would be very wrong indeed. From questions and conversations repeated again and again, I gained the conviction that the Canadians belong to the British Empire not merely out of habit, not only for practical considerations, but from a warm feeling of kinship. At the moment there is no trace whatsoever of leaning toward the United States. Western Canada at least appears to be free of jingoism and Germanophobia; the opinion of one German journalist who was welcomed everywhere in the kindest way possible can vouch for this perhaps only with partial authority. All the Germans living here, however, confirm these impressions for me. In eastern Canada it may be different. Out here, King Edward is very little on people's minds; when he is, his skill in external politics, his discretion in internal politics, and his personal calm and dignity assure him recognition from all sides. To be sure, the loyalty of western Canada appears to rest on two pillars, the removal of which could endanger it. The one is the awareness of being treated by England not as a daughter but as a sister, as a nearly independent ally. The nation considers itself grown up and would not tolerate any maternal interference. The other is that England will always have to bear the main expense for the Empire's armed services, for even though the patriotism of the Canadians for Greater Britain is genuine and warm, it will perhaps not stand the test of an all too heavy financial burden.

VII IRRIGATION

Calgary (Alberta) in August

Calgary is the capital of irrigation. It is of interest for many other reasons as well. Above all, it has sandstone pits nearby and makes good use of them; as a result its streets look stately and, for America, almost unusually solid. Furthermore, the streets are not so extravagantly wide as those in Winnipeg or Edmonton, perhaps because the city is closed in on three sides by hills. It lies exactly at the point where prairie and mountain country meet. This was the initial reason that the CPR set up a main station here, but it in itself also gave the city economic importance. Both factors appear to have attracted a higher social class to Calgary than one finds in other western Canadian cities. The whole strikes one as being not altogether English, yet more Canadian-English than American-English — if I am to characterize its "Englishness." While the other places look more or less like giant construction sites, Calgary is a real city. And yet it has grown just like the others during the last few years — from a population of 4,800 in 1901 to a population of 29,000 today.

Calgary is the capital of irrigation, and everybody talks about irrigation as though this were the only source of prosperity in the city. This is so partly because it still has some charm of novelty, partly because everybody is on the lookout whether, with all this prolific creation of new values, there might not be something in it somewhere for him personally, and partly because the irrigation system is an operational branch of the CPR to which Calgary looks up respectfully as its founder and main industry. I am enough of a heretic to express the conviction that Calgary would not have much less significance without irrigation than with it. The district to the east of the city is being irrigated and thereby opened up; this is indeed a tremendous blessing. But 150 kilometres both to the north and to the south, the most fertile and thriving land in all of western Canada is already dependent on the city. Farming communities have already been established for many years in the area to the north. The area to the south of Calgary, however, was until a short time ago still the realm of the cowboy. Here huge ranches extended along the tracks, and thousands of horses and tens of thousands of beef cattle grazed on the rich prairie grass. Today when you drive toward the south, you'll only occasionally see a small herd here and there; instead, large fields of the most magnificent winter wheat stretch out — "The wheat that has made Alberta famous," Alberta Red, the strain which at the present time is bringing the best price. Wheat is king, as the Canadian declares proudly, but here it is not an absolute monarch. This is the land of mixed farming. Forage crops of all kinds grow in profusion and, besides, the cattle can stay outside throughout the winter. For the "Chinook," the foehn from the Pacific, comes over the mountains; and all through the winter it keeps clearing away the ice and the snow in a matter of days. Large stretches are, of course, still prairie, yet regularly interspersed with huge black squares of freshly broken farmland. These two regions to the north and south of Calgary are worked without irrigation, and they alone would constitute an area sufficient to support a good-sized city and make it grow.

For a long time, the land east of Calgary was considered to be useless for agriculture, and not until the introduction of irrigation was it generally settled. From this fact developed a strong misconception of the role which irrigation plays in western Canada. Especially in the U.S.A. and Europe the idea is prevalent that an area, cultivation of which would be out of the question under natural conditions, is here being rendered fertile and suitable for settlement through irrigation. This is the case in Colorado, if I am not mistaken. Here in Alberta, however, the importance of irrigation has been wrongly assessed. No expert critic would nowadays deny that this whole part of the country is arable even without artificial irrigation. The CPR itself is not responsible for that false notion. Its employees and its publications stress again and again that irrigation in these parts is nothing more than an insurance against drought. The smart farmer will place as much value on it as he would on hail insurance. Whoever prefers to bear the risk can make do without hail insurance and thus, too, without irrigation. It is in the express interest of the CPR to make this point perfectly clear; because in almost two-thirds of all the land in question here and owned by them, artificial irrigation is, for technical reasons, unfeasible. As a matter of fact, the settling of non-irrigable land has kept pace with the settling of irrigable land. The farmers of the "dry" land prosper in the best possible way and are, to a man, just as satisfied with their acquisition as their neighbours are with their irrigated land. It is true, though, that they must apply basically different methods of cultivation. In the final analysis, you see, artificial irrigation does indeed mean something more than a safeguard against drought. It alone enables the farmer in this part of the country to have a mixed (therefore more intensive) farming operation. However, there are many farmers here who don't want to grow anything but grain, and they claim they don't need any artificial irrigation even in this area. Whether or not they are right is a much-disputed question which cannot possibly be answered by a layman. In most years the wheatfield is not irrigated, even on irrigable land. On the whole it can probably be said that, with appropriate farming methods, the farmer on "dry" land runs neither a much greater nor a much smaller risk than the farmer in other countries. The farmer with irrigation runs a little less than normal risk and can furthermore operate more intensively than his neighbour.

As part of the land subsidy paid by the government for the construction of the transcontinental line, the CPR received a continuous area of 1,200,000 hectares immediately to the east of Calgary. This is the irrigation area. The water needed is channelled from the Bow River into a wide main-canal which, 10 kilometres below Calgary, divides into side-canals which subdivide again into numerous branches. From the side-canals the company conducts the water to the highest point on the boundary of each irrigable farm. From this point the farmer then runs ditches along the land to be irrigated, and from them he cuts furrows across the thirsty field with his plough or hoe, if necessary. The entire huge area belonging to the CPR is divided into three sections of approximately equal size. Of these, only the western one is settled and irrigated. About 80% of this section has already been sold, of which half lies too high for irrigation. Although the years since 1905, when irrigation began, have not received the heaviest precipitation in this area, even the buyers of the high-lying land are full of praise for the land and the climate and their crops. Yet, their property is not much cheaper than the irrigable land, $20 as compared to $25 [per acre]. The price of water, incidentally, is set by the Dominion authority. The CPR, just like the government, has been trying hard to get American settlers in particular, and the great majority of the farmers on the irrigable land seems to come from the U.S. Danes who, as you know, bring along experience in irrigation from their home-country, just like the Americans, are also represented in great numbers. It seems the Company is going to increase its activity with regard to the recruiting of immigrants in Europe as well. Next year, one or two Russian-German farmers from the Rosthern area are to be sent to Bessarabia to lure some of their fellow-countrymen here. I have reason to believe that German Nationals also will show up again in their native land on behalf of the CPR in order to demonstrate by their own prosperity how much a farmer can extract from the Canadian soil.

An interesting Italian project is presently in preparation. Italian capitalists have purchased somewhat more than 600 acres in the irrigation area, which they propose to divide into farms of about 65 acres each and lease them to Italian peasants according to the 50:50 system used in Tuscany. In the centre a church and a schoolhouse are built, and the farms will lie around them like spokes of a wheel. Of course every leaseholder will leave the colony after some time to take up a homestead or, if he has already saved enough, to buy a farm. Each time, replacement is to come from Italy. For the purpose of this project, I am assured, is not a financial but a patriotic one. In Canada as well as in the States, Italian immigration so far does not have a good name; it consists almost exclusively of workers from southern Italy. Now they want to show the New World that there are also Italians with a higher culture, and they therefore want to bring over peasants from central and northern Italy. Whether or not these capitalists also intend to make a little money in this remains to be seen. Not long ago, the Italian government sent a university professor from Rome over here to examine the conditions, an indication that this project is meant to be merely an experiment and the beginning of colonization on a larger scale.

VIII IRRIGATION — ON THE PRAIRIE

Calgary (Alberta) in August

At several points of its large irrigation area, the CPR operates demonstration farms. This is done partly to set an example for the settlers in the development of suitable agricultural methods, and partly to show prospective buyers what the soil and irrigation can do. I have visited the model farm near Strathmore and have seen a number of private farms in the same area on dry as well as on irrigated land. The model farm covers a little more than 600 acres and is, of course, cultivated in the most careful way. First priority is assigned to those crops which could not be grown in this area without irrigation. These include especially trees, and more important for the farmer, clover, alfalfa, and other forage crops. Besides vegetables of all kinds, for the first time they experimented with sugar beets this year; a neighbouring farmer is also growing several hundred hectares of these and, because they seem to do very well, the construction of a sugar refinery is in the planning. Of course, the model farm also grows grain crops; but this is done, at least this year, without irrigation. Nevertheless, I was shown oats that were well filled and over seven feet high, excellent barley and rather good wheat. The other farms I toured grew largely forage crops if irrigated, and the "dry" ones grew almost exclusively oats and wheat. Since the winter wheat in southern Alberta was destroyed to a great extent this year by spring frosts, there was a lot of re-seeding, usually oats, at the end of April or the beginning of May. I found one such mixed field — because part of the winter wheat comes up anyway — which, even though on a non-irrigable elevation, stood better than all the fields in lower-lying areas where artificial irrigation was possible (although it has not been used this year, as I already mentioned). The farmer's wife, sitting on the binder pulled by four horses and cutting the rich harvest, told of many reasons why her husband and other owners of "dry" farms in this area considered it more produtive than the irrigable land.

Certainly this would not generally apply; however, I mention it as typical of the rosy contentment of the entire Canadian farm population. Throughout my whole journey I didn't find a single farmer who would complain about the soil or the climate or the yield; only the best side is stressed at all times, and temporary misfortune is overlooked with a smile. Furthermore, the natural growing conditions on the farm of the person asked are always better than, or at least as good as, those of his neighbours, and the region is superior "to any other region on earth." Of course, a lot of this is American boastfulness, but it also reflects a terrific optimism and proud belief in the maxim, "If you want a thing done, do it yourself!" The aforementioned farmer's wife — it would probably not do to call the lady-driver of a four-horse binder a reaper — is also worthy of mention because, in the preceding article, the Londoners came off so very badly.

For two years ago the young woman was still a sales clerk in a London ladies'-wear shop, then ventured off by herself into the New World, married an American farmer, and came up here last summer with him. Did she like it better here than in the big city? My God, you should have seen her eyes shine with zest for life! Never would she go back to the smoke and fog of the Thames! The work on a farm is hard, that is true, and she had never known what real work was, but the work is precisely the very best thing about it! Then she pushed her hair from her forehead with a slender hand and the gesture of a lady and drove vigorously on, cutting down the grain and turning the corner of the field with the greatest precision.

I got to know the other type of English immigrant on the same evening. — "A room by yourself?" said the lady hotelkeeper. "That you can only have during winter. But because you are a foreigner I'll give you a bed for yourself." Both my roommates proved to be interesting fellows. A handsome chap, the Englishman, with a black moustache in his narrow face; and the tastefully simple tie looked almost coquettish above his worn Wild-West outfit. Had been a gentleman's coachman in London, came into a small inheritance, and figured that in Canada one could become a rich man with it. Went up into the area of the North Saskatchewan River and started to raise horses. But the city-boy was not interested in working horses: it had to be purebloods, racing horses, if possible. Of course, the venture fell through. "I am just not a good manager," he said with an elegantly resigned smile. Now he is glad to have found a job in a livery stable, but is mad at Canada and says — and this is literally the only exception to the previously mentioned rule — the notion that farmers get rich is only a figment of the imagination; if they would work as hard somewhere else, they could get further ahead. This, of course, is nonsense because where "somewhere else" is everybody given 160 acres to start out with? . . . The other fellow I shared the room with was a type in himself, and a good contrast to his bedfellow. A broad-shouldered young giant, an eastern Canadian of Scottish descent, and for a few years now a cowboy in southernmost Alberta. The ranch where he had been working was now being divided up, the wild prairie being broken up, and the farmer, with his more advanced agriculture, was replacing the free herds of thousands of horses and beef cattle. The cowboys were let go. The man was a victim of economic progress; he hadn't come into, nor wasted, an inheritance, but he complained about neither the country nor the way of the world. Roared with laughter and shouted: "The finest country on the face of the earth!" Wants to hire himself out as a farmhand for a year, learn about agriculture, and put some money away. He will then take up a homestead or, if he has saved enough, buy a small plot of irrigated land. These are the people that conquer life because they know how to learn from it!

The next day I rode westward across the prairie, under the horse's hoofs nothing but the grey-green sod — hardly confined by the rolling hills ahead of me. The wind sings through the dry grass and, high above, pushes the brightly laughing clouds along. The horse pricks up its ears, stretches out in a long stride, and now we gallop along in a race with the song of the wind and the fleeting clouds. Already the first rise is reached, I give the horse free rein, and up it goes like blazes. . .; then, a jerk, and we stand: there in the remote, hazy distance, for the very first time — the Rocky Mountains! A long range of massive, wild summits, battletorn peaks; the name "Rocky Mountains" gains meaning. The eyes almost want to jump over to the object of so many a youthful dream and wildly intoxicating fantasy. Only slowly they become tired and lower themselves, still so full of memories as well as of the new sight . . . there, — what is that? These are no dreams, there they actually stand right below me on the prairie: one, two, three, ten, a dozen of the pointed high tents — Redskins! Winnetou! Leatherstocking! Here they are in the flesh, and there is their encampment. The first thought that comes into my mind is funny: My gosh, I am standing up-wind! and I have to laugh. No hero of my childhood would have approached the Indians in this manner; one creeps toward the tent from down-wind! But then the question occurs to me: what are they doing here, far away from any reservation? Are they on the warpath? Not a soul is around. But what is that thing — it is painted red and blue — that is flashing behind the chief's tepee? I take a few steps to the side and now I can see it: it is not a gun-barrel as the romantic reader might have thought, but — a hay-tedder. Agricultural implements in an Indian camp! My innermost feelings are hurt and shocked by such decadence! But, in any case, there is no doubt, they are "on the peace-path" and, leisurely, I ride down the hill.

Several big wolf-dogs emerge from the tepees, but only one deems me worthy of a warning howl. A few brown children peep out from a very small tent and are royally amused as I attempt a conversation. Their laughter causes several women to stick their heads out of the tents; they understand as little English as I do Indian, and two men who finally crawl into the daylight also just shrug their shoulders and settle down again on the ground in stoic indifference — something which I recognize with satisfaction, from my old books about Indians, as being "genuine." A pretty girl of eight or ten has a belt embroidered with glass beads; I show her a coin and give her to understand that I would like to have the belt. The coin makes her brown eyes shine and her fingers dance back and forth on her belt, but in the end she doesn't dare. So I let her lead me to the tepee from which she fetches her mother. The latter contemplates the coin doubtfully and then calls a man from the adjacent tent who finally says something in broken English.

They are Blackfoot Indians, once the most savage red warriors of the northern prairie. Now they have left the reservations in single groups and hired themselves out for haying, as they do every year. Other men know good English, he makes clear to me, but they are out working. The men here also wear ordinary clothes, just like those one sees in the city, but two of them in addition have colourful blankets wrapped around their shoulders, despite the heat. Their hair hangs down in front of their shoulders in two black braids. The children are dressed in simple red-brown little frocks

Courtesy of Saskatchewan Archives

Indian camp, Alberta

that suit their dark faces and big eyes. The women wear brighter skirts in red and brown colours and, as far as their attire is concerned, could easily be taken for gypsy women. Around the women's and children's necks hang primitive necklaces made of brass beads and two among them have necklaces made of glass beads. A few women inside the tents are cooking the evening meal, small pieces of meat in a grey-brown broth, or potatoes in a garish green one. The others lie sleepily around inside, stretched out on the many-coloured blankets.

Later, as I ride on, I pass by the horses of the camp, about three dozen of them — shaggy, scrawny beasts for the most part — tended by a few brown boys. Then I am off farther to the south — a small farm, vegetables, beets, and oats. Two young Americans from eastern Ohio — the one's name of course is Meyer, born on the Rhine — started farming here last spring. Otherwise everything within a wide radius is still open prairie. For a long time I ride along one of the irrigation canals. Two dots appear in the distance and are fast approaching. They are two young Indians, a boy and a girl, about sixteen years old or maybe eighteen; brother and sister, no doubt about that. Both have fine features, unusually narrow for Indians and, as they trot along on the opposite bank, I have to admire their magnificent bearing. The girl sits in the saddle like a brown-skinned contessa.

We stop abreast of one another and the brother inquires about a shallow spot to water their horses. I give him the information, but he looks at the irrigation water somewhat warily: "Did your horse drink?" — "Yes, it did." I then ask him where they come from and where they are going. They are not half breeds as I had thought for a moment, but belong to the camp I just passed and have been visiting a farmer beyond Strathmore. Is the Chief their father perhaps? — Not this one but Chief . . . , and he gurgles a name I don't dare to spell out despite his repeating it twice for me; let the reader also gurgle something and he will hit the mark.

So far the girl has, of course, kept silent. Now she softly whispers something to her brother and he asks, obviously with no great pleasure but obediently: "You no cowboy? . . . Foreign hat." — "No, I come from across the great water, from Germany." He smiles and says with an admiring gesture of his hand: "Oh, oh, far away!"

To the question: "Ever heard of Germany?" he is silent. But the girl says with a smile, "I know!" and is immediately startled by her own audacity. "What's your name?" I turn to her. She puts her hand on her brother's arm and he answers: "Uglaw." — "Her name?" — "Yes, Uglaw," she repeats herself and it almost looks as though she is quite proud of her name. "What does it mean in English?" And she prompts him: "Prairie Flower."

However, in every second Indian story there is a brown beauty by the name of "Prairie Flower" and I probe further: "Which Prairie flower?" She points at a sort of dandelion, a great yellow-petalled star with a dark-red eye, and the brother confirms it: "This one here." — "The prettiest flowers on the prairie, they and you!" She laughs delightedly, quite unselfconsciously. I ask her whether she went to an Indian school. She says no and and the brother says: "But *little* sister will go," and the big sister shows with her hand how small the little one is. Where would I find the next bridge? — A mile upstream. "Good bye!" — "Good bye!" and in a beautiful smooth gallop they ride on.

IX CANADIAN MORMONS

Lethbridge (Alberta) Early September

Canada's older but much smaller and lesser known irrigation area lies near Lethbridge in the southernmost part of Alberta, not far from the American border. It is almost exclusively settled by Mormons. These two facts have been lumped together, and thence the conclusion has been drawn that the credit for having introduced the principle of irrigation from the States into Canada should go to the Mormons. This belief is propagated with great pride in the U.S. and also expressed in literature. Whether this is correct or not is difficult to determine. But the Mormons were in any case familiar with irrigation from Utah and therefore especially inclined and especially qualified to apply the same system in their new Canadian settlement.

In 1887, when the first small Mormon community came up in their ox-carts, founded the little hamlet of Cardston, and began to till the land in these parts for the first time, everything down here in southern Alberta was still open prairie. Because they hadn't known anything but irrigation back home, they got to work immediately, digging a canal from the St. Mary River, meaning to water the young fields artificially. The irrigation just wouldn't function, however, and the people had to learn that not every region is suited to the Mormon system; they also learned that not every region needs it. The old ditch has long since filled in, but the people of Cardston have developed a thriving agriculture and have become prosperous. The only things that won't grow readily in the area are trees; apart from that, not only cereal grains and forage crops but also any kind of vegetables and sugar beets grow well here. In 1907, a typical year I am assured, Cardston had almost the highest precipitation in the Province of Alberta and it was well distributed: little rain in spring and a lot in summer.

In the meantime, in the early Nineties came the great drought which was a major contributing factor in slowing down the settlement of Canada. At that time, several communities in Alberta — not down here but between Macleod and Calgary — and also several farmers began to dig small irrigation ditches on their own. This eventually led the Dominion Government to investigate whether the land might not be suitable for a larger-scale irrigation system, and they found two districts where this was the case. I have already reported about the great irrigation facilities east of the City of Calgary. The second area lending itself to systematic irrigation extended to the south of Lethbridge along a large Blood Indian Reserve and about halfway up to Cardston. Most of the land in this area had been deeded to the Alberta Railway Company as a subsidy. Now a subsidiary was founded which, by the end of 1900, had built an extensive irrigation system, the water for which was taken from the St. Mary River. At the present time some 120,000 hectares can be watered artificially.

It is perhaps more accurate to say that the Mormons were brought here by the irrigation than vice versa. For it was not until the installation had been completed and was in operation that there was a greater influx of Mormons, mainly from Utah and Idaho. The people I spoke with all say: the church sent us up here to break new land and to open a new field to our church. In reality, it evidently was a group of Mormon capitalists, some of whom are extremely rich, who wanted to set up a sugar plant here and, for this purpose, had the necessary number of farmers sent up with the aid of the church. The Knight Sugar Company with a capital of one million dollars initially acquired 120,000 hectares of land, 50,000 of which they have since sold. Of their remaining property a great portion is ranch land, presently running 15,000 head of cattle and 2,000 horses. Sugar production in the last few years amounted to five million pounds and seems to be paying off well. The only thing they complain about is the difficulty of getting enough beets. In 1908, the farmers of the district planted approximately 600 hectares of beets and the company itself 400 hectares. This year the farmers thought wheat would be more profitable, and the beet fields were reduced by 250 hectares, so that the plant had to increase its own production by as much. Both suffer extremely from shortage of labour. I talked to several farmers who had grown beets as long as their children were small. They then stopped because paid hands are expensive and the adult members of the family are reluctant to work in the beet fields, and are probably less suited for it. The plant management complains very much about the fact that the farmers fail to cultivate their beet fields carefully; it is indeed a bad sign that their yields, eight tons per acre on the average, do not exceed those of the plant although the growing of beet crops lends itself so readily to a small operation. The plant employs only whites for the inside jobs, but mainly Japanese, some Indians, and a few Chinese for field work. During harvest time, several hundred Indians help; they always hire out with their whole family and are said to be really good workers.

In this area as well, irrigation is considered mainly an insurance against drought; in a year like the present one, hardly any use is made of it, at least not in agriculture. Of course, it always comes in handy for the little garden and the few trees around the house. Even in drier years only a portion of the beet fields is irrigated. The views on the merits and demerits of irrigation in sugar beet cultivation are sharply divided. What it comes down to is probably this: irrigation makes the beets grow larger, but reduces their sugar content somewhat. The soil, in any case, appears to be highly suitable for beet production and it is no less fertile for cereal and forage crops. The fields, as far as they haven't been harvested yet, offer a magnificent sight; alfalfa, which is extensively grown here, is the most beautiful. Cattle-raising is being done to quite a large extent and with excellent results.

There is no doubt that the Mormons are doing very well here but, considering their rich agricultural returns, they don't appear to be as prosperous as one would expect after visiting other parts of western

Canada. The reason for that is perhaps the great simplicity of their way of life; they look more like farmers than the American farmer usually does. In no way are they poor, and the prosperity needed for rustic comfort seems very evenly distributed. Only the general rise to riches that tends to characterize the more efficient Canadian farmer is not evident here and, although this is certainly neither a necessary nor always a gratifying result of human endeavour, it cannot be replaced by the fact that, among the great mass of little people, only a handful make it to the top and become capitalists worth millions. Another reason why the prosperity of most Mormons remains within modest bounds could possibly be the extremely heavy demands, financial as well as personal, made on them by their church.

The Mormons, as is well known, tithe to their church in keeping with the old Jewish law. "At least that's what they ought to do," says one of their elders, a farmer and owner of a livery stable who is driving me across the country, "but some people use somewhat unorthodox methods in their accounting." Out of the tithing money schools and churches are maintained, and the poor aided. The rest of the money goes to Salt Lake City, the capital of the Mormon State of Utah. Besides paying tithe, each male is expected to devote two to five years of his life to missionary work. This, of course, he usually does in his youth, but not always. My companion, for instance, waited until his sons were old enough to look after the farm by themselves and then he went off. For this missionary work the church pays nothing at all. Missionaries are expected to move around without any cash and to rely completely on the charity of the people, not of fellow-believers of course, as there are hardly any outside of the Mormon colony. The missionary's family is responsible for his special needs, such as clothing, travel money, etc., and perhaps even to supplement charity that might not be forthcoming. Every community also has a so-called mission farm which is worked by all the members of the colony, with the proceeds going to finance the missionaries who have no means of their own whatsoever. Instead of this mission farm, the town of Raymond which I also visited runs an OPERA HOUSE, a popular name for variety and cinematographic theatres in the American small town. One should therefore not expect to see "Aïda" or "Tannhäuser" in such an opera house. I suggested a performance of [Meyerbeer's] "The Prophet," and my companion decided to take the matter under advisement. For the time being, the opera house is used mainly as a dance hall and rolier-skating rink, and Raymond's mission coffers are said to be well filled at all times.

Polygamy, as is common knowledge, has been abolished for years. However, everybody with whom I discussed this assured me that their faith in the piety as well as religious superiority of polygamy has in no way been shaken, but that the Church demands obedience to the laws of the State. My aforementioned companion expounded at great length on the following reasons for polygamy. Firstly, if God hadn't destined us for polygamy, why then would He allow the reproductiveness of the male to go on longer than that of the female and without periodic interruptions? The average woman remained reproductive to the age of 45, the man to the age of 60. From this viewpoint, therefore, two women would be enough if the second marriage were entered into approximately fifteen years and six months after the first wedding day. Secondly, God commanded the people to multiply as much as possible; ergo, the more women, the better! In the hereafter every man would be reunited with his whole family, and he who then was surrounded in the heavenly train by the greatest number of children would be rewarded with the highest glory by God and his angels. This idea conjured up for me the picture of a military parade, but I prudently kept it to myself.

Divorce, adultery, and prostitution proved that a man was not meant to get by with one wife. In Utah, a farmer often has a few fields near this village and a few fields near that village. Would it then not be the most natural thing in the world to have also a wife in each place? I thought this very pleasant for the man, at least as long as all his wives were young. But what was the wife to do while the husband was trailing about, for weeks, with the other two, three, perhaps eight or ten "better halves" or "better twelfths"? Could not the woman, too, have feelings of desire? — "The wife will simply have to sacrifice herself for her faith!"

"But is it just if only the wife makes the sacrifices and the husband enjoys all the amenities of faith?" — "Amenities?" the worthy minister flared up. "Is it an amenity when a man like my friend Johnson has to feed and raise 126 children!" . . . "What is such a man?"

"A Company commander." (The word slipped out of my mouth.)

"No, he is a hero of the faith!"

I couldn't help carrying the dispute further: "But then he can also grow sugar beets under the cheapest possible conditions! The fact that the Mormon states have developed the largest beet production in America appears to be a direct result of their religion, their polygamy, their abundance of children!"

"Indeed," was the answer, "this is the reward our Lord has given us!"

X GENERAL REMARKS

Lethbridge (Alberta) Early September

May I add a few general remarks to the specific observations which seemed worth reporting during my short visit to the Canadian Northwest. The Canadian government constantly makes the most extraordinary efforts to attract farmers — especially experienced ones with capital — into the country. Their efforts in regard to American immigrants have already been mentioned. Not only do they maintain dozens of agencies and distribute tens of thousands of advertising leaflets in the U.S.; every year, agents of the Dominion Government travel the circuit of the larger fairs in the northwestern States and conjure up, in the most glowing colours, before the farmers' eyes and ears a picture of the newest land of unlimited opportunities. In Europe one tries to win immigrants from the following countries: Great Britain, Germany, Scandinavia, France, Holland, and Belgium. South- and East-Europeans are lately looked upon as non-desirable additions. From several quarters, particularly from Mr. Walker, the Inspector of Immigration in Winnipeg, I heard the complaint that it was very difficult to get German settlers because the government of the Kaiser worked against the Canadian recruiting effort.

This position taken by the German government I find completely proper. A growing industrial nation can never have too many people. Least of all can we do without those persons the Canadian government covets: our farmers. An industrial nation can never have enough farmers. It must draw out of the soil as much food as possible — in quantity and in quality. On a soil such as that in Germany this can only be done through an agricultural economy. Just at this moment when the farmers themselves are beginning to recognize again their true foe, their sworn enemy, Naumann's slogan should be taken up by all Germany: Farm upon farm as far as the Russian border! [Friedrich Naumann was founder of the German Democratic Party, and a member of the Reichstag in the Weimar Republic.]

We certainly can't spare any farmers for Canada, but neither can we spare workers. The Dominion Government does not want industrial workers anyway, and, in fact, has no use for them. It is pleased to get farmhands so long as there are no independent farmers to be had. Our farm workers are the least to blame for emigrating, at least as long as our large landowners can reconcile their patriotic sentiment with bringing Poles and Galicians into Germany, rather than keeping German workers on the land by paying them better wages. Only at such time as inner colonization is practised, not only *against* the Poles but *for* the Germans — that kind of inner colonization which means democratization of our agriculture — will our farm labourer find a place and a lasting home on German soil, too.

* * *

It was not the purpose of these letters to describe Canadian conditions in general. They could only tell what their author saw with his own eyes during his short trip. Naturally these were the areas along, or not far away from, the railway lines. Therefore the reports were mainly about farmers who have been living in the country for ten or even twenty years, or about those who arrived later but with capital. As a rule, the later immigrants without capital had to go farther inside the country. Their soil is probably not worse, but as long as they have to spend a lot of money and time to reach the nearest station, their economic progress is bound to be relatively slow. It is true, though, that new track is being laid constantly and with admirable energy. Nonetheless, on the average, the situation of the combined western Canadian farmers would certainly not look quite as bright as the situation in the areas I have visited. Land prices vary today almost exclusively according to the greater or lesser distance from a railway station.

The farmer who has made good would much rather talk about his success than about the sweat, the privation, the hunger which this success has cost him. An optimist through and through and always looking forward like a real or, in any case, a quickly assimilated American, he doesn't like to wallow in unhappy memories. But once one succeeds in getting him on to this topic, then the bright present stands out against the grey background of long years of suffering and want. He who lives in a good brick building today, once with his wife and children had to freeze through long icy winters in a miserable shack made of tar paper. He who now eats his fill three times a day and still takes money to the bank, once had to toil day-in day-out until his back was sore, and had to rack his brains merely to produce a few slices of dry bread for hungry mouths. And how many there were, thousands and tens of thousands, who perished or, giving up the struggle, left the country! No report could be made on all those who are no longer here. Anyone who was able to hold out till the last good decade came along is very well-off today. But can bad years not happen again? The people out here have learned a lot in the meantime and they won't go under even in bad years. Nevertheless, progress cannot always remain so spectacular, and whoever starts out farming today would be reckless indeed if he were to take the Canadian boom of the last decade as a basis for his calculations.

The industrial workers are the ones who should be warned most emphatically against emigrating to Canada. There is no demand for them here at all, and the wages in relation to the high prices are really not good. Besides, a person without working capital cannot start farming, even in spite of the free homestead, and a person with capital will not get much return from it without farming experience. Farming needs to be learned and is learned less easily than the city-dweller generally assumes. The failure of many English colonists I previously told about serves as a warning example. The experience of the European farmer, moreover, does not necessarily suffice for a Canadian farm. Working as a farmhand for one or more years offers the best opportunity for learning how to farm in this country, but this is a very hard apprenticeship, full of privation; and the city worker, who in our country doesn't want to go out onto the land even in the worst of times, will probably not last long here, either.

However, if somebody has made up his mind to become King Edward's subject, he should never, and *under no circumstances,* buy Canadian land from Europe. Among the land companies which look for a market in the Old World there are also some German-Canadian names. People here, to the last man, have an extremely bad opinion of them; stories are told which I will not repeat here simply because I have had no chance to verify them. But in general it can be said that land companies do not have very desirable farms for sale, because they can only own such land as is neither reserved by the Government for homesteads nor owned by the railways. By and large the railways have the best land, because under their subvention agreements they didn't have to accept poor land. Nevertheless, one should buy nothing that one hasn't seen, even from the railway companies. People who are so naive as to buy land from a distance will always be offered the poorest land. This, of course, more definitely applies to the land companies than to the railways.

A man with a capital of less than 25,000 to 30,000 Marks should not even think of buying a farm. He can only take up a homestead. Open land will still be available in Canada for many years. Up to now there are still homesteads to be had even near new stretches of railway. In one respect the homesteads along the Grand Trunk Pacific merit the greatest notice because this line, unlike the two others, received its subsidy in cash. Therefore their land office confines itself to recommending suitable areas for settlement, especially those suitable for homesteads. The land offices of the CPR and the Canadian Northern do this only on the side; their main concern is of course to sell their own land. Anyone wanting to take up a homestead needs an initial capital of at least 1,000 Marks. But then he would have to start out in such a "Wild-West" manner that even a modest German farmer or worker would not find it to his liking. One cannot manage well with less than 5,000 Marks. Even then progress will be very slow if there is a lack of that capital which is most valuable to the Canadian farmer: able-bodied sons!

Whoever has some capital would do best to start right out determined to do mixed farming. No knowledgeable person is in any doubt that, even on Saskatchewan's young land, the exclusive — and therefore primitive — cultivation of wheat will in the near future be as unprofitable for the privately owned operation as it is already today for the national economy as a whole. Generally speaking, the Province of Alberta at present is the land with more mixed farming, and any beginner with capital can profit by the experience of his neighbours which, in Saskatchewan, he will have to gain by himself. Obviously, a more diversified farm operation has to be close to a railway station and as near as possible to a town. Homesteads are no longer available in such locations; here land must be bought. It does not follow, of course, that land companies do not have the best land in the vicinity of towns. As a rule, however, the railway companies are to be preferred among the land agents. For they would do themselves a disservice if they gave the settler land which would not yield a profit, or if they asked an uneconomic price. For them the real estate business is a means to an end and their "end" is the freight business. The more the farmer prospers, the more freight he will supply. As far as I could see, the Canadian railway companies really let themselves be guided by this principle.

Western Canada is not a land of milk and honey. But if one is willing to work from dawn to dusk one probably can today get further ahead here than in most other countries. In spite of this, it is undesirable for us as Germans to send more people across the Atlantic than unfortunately already have gone. What we have to supply are finished products and capital. There is more than enough room in western Canada for both. Today a visitor to this country can practically tell only of agricultural phenomena. The spectacular progress naturally means correspondingly favourable commercial and industrial prospects. In this respect there is ample room also for Germany, but the question is how to get in when the door is closed. The tariff war has to be ended before we can enjoy the abundance of this newest land of unlimited opportunities. The people here work; they have as little interest in questions of trade politics as they have in questions of world politics. For this reason it is not often possible to learn their opinions on the German-Canadian tariff war. Naturally, the desire to see it settled is unanimous, but this desire is too vague to carry any weight. Only one thing may be worthy of note — everyone who was at all interested in this question stated this thought in one way or another: Germany was first to deem it necessary to make some changes in its trade relations with Canada, and therefore Germany ought to take the first step toward reconciliation!

COHNSTAEDT'S ITINERARY 1909

AV-Services, University of Regina

XI THROUGH BRITISH COLUMBIA

"That is the old homeland," blond little Miss Florence exclaimed when she heard, high up at the Crowsnest Pass, that our train had just crossed the border between Alberta and British Columbia, and her eyes sparkled.

The old homeland? —Just an hour ago she had told us it was only three years since her father and mother and the whole family came from England and settled down in the capital of British Columbia. And already she calls it "the old homeland"? With all the enthusiasm her English blood could muster she explained, in answer to my surprised question, the reasons for this feeling of belonging. Yet, while one easily believes a pretty mouth and two shiny eyes for the moment, this exclamation gains full and lasting meaning for me only now that I have seen some of British Columbia for myself. For the "British" in the name of this Canadian province is no hollow word. Not only is this province different from another Columbia but also from the rest of the Canadian Dominion: naturally it differs from French Quebec, certainly from Ontario which is said to have developed a new stereotype of Canadian, and it also differs strikingly and sharply from the American Canadian provinces of the West. It should really be called "English-Columbia." It is the English character of the people that is most obvious and indeed characteristic. British Columbia is making good economic progress, but it is not surging ahead to the same extent as the prairie provinces. Hunger for the dollar does not dominate everything to the exclusion of all else; a civilized enjoyment of what the newly earned dollars can buy also has its place. Indeed, people here almost pride themselves less on their new achievements than on the old ways which they brought over with them. Immigration of all nationalities — Europeans, Asians and above all Americans by the tens of thousands — has taken place, of course, and is continuing in British Columbia as well. However, the English were here first, the stream from the mother-country has never dried up and, to this date, they have remained the core of the population. They feel at home here in this English dependency on the Pacific Ocean and, along with the pretty Miss who considered the prairie provinces all too "American Wild-West," they all feel: "this is the old homeland."

The prairie provinces had to be reached by endless treks from the East or the South. Their settlement, therefore, was long in coming and, when the time arrived, the regions in the East and in the South were developed enough to do their own colonizing. It was Canadians and Americans who took possession of the Northwest, Manitoba, Saskatchewan, and Alberta.

The land on the coast was naturally accessible by sea. England's seafaring sons entered here directly. British Columbia was still a British colony until 1871. But it is the land formation in this coastal province that makes it essentially different from the other provinces. There are no open stretches of endless prairie land here; from the Alberta border to the Pacific Ocean one finds high mountain ranges, lower mountain ranges, and narrow mountain valleys. Because the arable land is limited, the government does not give it away for nothing, and because it is densely timbered from one end to the other, the high cost of clearing must be added to the purchase price. A person without means does not find a homestead here where he can work his way up to prosperity; only one who invests capital in the land may work it, but of course he can also expect handsome returns. The farmer doesn't grow grain crops or raise livestock, nor is he likely ever to do so; rather, he grows fruit and vegetables or is in the dairy business. Even where British Columbia's valleys are at all arable, settlement naturally progresses at a slower pace than on the open prairie. Among British Columbia's production industries, agriculture, measured in terms of its productivity, is only in fourth place. Ahead of it are mining, lumbering, and fishing. All this explains the diversity in the population. The farmers are fruit growers; almost all are Englishmen, or Easterners who arrived here with money. The foreign immigrants, including the Americans, have largely remained labourers, especially miners and lumberjacks, or they live in the cities. Many have become well-off, even rich, yet they are not looked up to as leaders in the community.

The great majority of travellers see practically nothing of British Columbia's activities. For the mainline of the Canadian Pacific Railway, the CPR, crosses the province first through high mountains and then through desolate rocky valleys. The high mountains are what the traveller is looking for here, the Canadian Alps. Yet British Columbia's life is in the side valleys which he passes by. Half a dozen of these side valleys have already been opened up by the trains and steamships of the CPR. A network of branch lines, crossing the country diagonally from the south-east, makes it easy enough to get to see almost the entire settled area of the province. Withal, this route is of such great scenic beauty that it should not be used only by settlers and travelling businessmen.

Starting from Lethbridge, the central point of southernmost Alberta, the Crowsnest Pass line runs at first across dry prairie into which the St. Mary River has dug its bed to a depth of 100 metres or so. The tortuous bends of the river and the enormous clefts on both sides bear witness to the wild force which has sought its way. Never has the power of the water been more vividly impressed upon me than here where it is capable of interrupting the endless expanse of the prairie with its deep cuts and gorges. And never did the prairie fascinate me more strongly than here where it stretches out beyond the clefts and gorges in majestic indifference without end — and seemingly without beginning. Fields are still scarce down here; it is the last retreat of the great ranches. Smaller and larger herds of beef, hundreds of little black dots, are strewn here and there across the wide prairie. There they lie and stand about feeding and chewing their cud. From time to time a group of grazing horses gallop off at the sight of the train. At one time I count about 300 of them. They are closely huddled together at the centre; at the flanks they race along in loose formation, a magnificently gracious picture and yet touched by a hint of tragedy, and when I analyze my feelings I think of it as the flight of the masterless animals after the death ride near Mars la Tour [in the Franco-Prussian War].

In the west and southwest the wild peaks and masses of the Rocky Mountains gradually emerge from the mist and, a few kilometres to the north, the bleak heights of the Porcupine Hills accompany us. "Porcupine Hills" — the name only takes on meaning as we are about to leave them behind and see the last slope spiked with isolated gaunt spruce trees. The whole hill range must once have looked like that; this was already a come-down from the former mountain forest, and now forest fires turn even the mildly ironic name into a legend. It is a fitting prelude to our drive through the Rocky Mountains which we are now entering. For the dominant impression of the mountain ride across the Crowsnest Pass is not of the mountains — beautiful though they rise up on both sides — initially comparable in height and shape to the Bavarian foothills, later roughly to the Kaisergebirge. Most dominant is the depressing sight of burnt forests. Wide stretches are of course still fully timbered with magnificent conifers, but they only seem to reflect what their neighbouring areas once looked like, and they again seem to herald the fate of the remaining forest. At least one third of the forest stand visible from the train has fallen victim to the fires of many years. The branches and all the boughs have disappeared, and merely a few dried-out little twigs twist on the trunks which remain standing here in the mountains, burnt-out and charred.

To the left the Turtle Mountain towers high up, a real wide turtle back; and now we cross a huge field of rubble, a mile wide and twice as long, where six years ago the mountains buried an entire town and 80 living souls. The mountains here on either side of the Crowsnest Pass bear enormous deposits of coal. Every few minutes the train stops at a small mining town. The entrails of the turtle, too, consist of wide veins of the "black diamond" and, starting from Frank, a mine had been driven into them. With typical American carelessness the shoring timbers had repeatedly been removed from the exhausted tunnels and used again further on. Gradually, the steep mountain was so deeply hollowed out that there was an overhang inside; and one night the entire front slope, 400 to 500 metres high, collapsed with a terrible thundering roar into itself and onto the valley, When the teams of the neighbouring towns arrived at dawn, they found nothing but an expanse of rocks, stones and rubble where only the day before there had been a thriving mining town. On the edge, however, a little child was crouching on a heap of rubble, howling and crying for father and mother; he was the only survivor of the town of Frank.

On the same site a new Frank has long since risen and in the pits ton after ton is being mined. "Do they now at least leave the supporting timber standing?" I asked a miner. "Partly," was the answer; "but not for the most part. The engineers assure us there is no danger of a further cave-in."

But did these engineers foresee the first collapse? They may be right, yet the traveller admires the brave people who have resettled right next to the ruins under which their neighbours and friends lie buried.

The same undaunted courage was shown by the people of Fernie, the little town that fell victim to a gigantic forest fire the year before last. Already the houses are rebuilt or are nearing completion — at least the larger ones — and the enthusiasm with which the visitor is informed of the significance of the place and its bright future has no equal in all Canada. Fernie, which claims to have a population of 3500, is a coal mining centre, and a long row of coke furnaces glows high in the night. When we come to stay overnight it is the evening of Labour Day. Canada like the U.S. has a Labour Day, an obligatory day of rest and a holiday declared by the government. The chief significance of the holiday lies in the fact that it always falls on a weekday. On Sundays, as you know, not only is the consumption of alcohol forbidden, but theatres, concerts, and even sports activities are also prohibited by police order. Thus the Labour Day and one or two patriotic holidays are the only "Sundays" in the joyful sense in which we understand this word. Sports competitions and entertainments fill the afternoon; the Labour Syndicate organizes them, but the entire population participates. In the evening a happy but oddly quiet crowd strolls through the streets. Now and then a few tipsy guys are singing, but nowhere do I see a drunk, nowhere any rowdiness or mischief. What has become of the notorious mining camps of the Wild West? My feelings waver between admiration for the progress of civilization and a certain disappointment that it is my fate to follow in its wake.

But it is more lively in the saloons. Gruff, rough fellows crowd around the bar, cursing, yelling, chewing, and spitting the tobacco juice over three heads; only the gun in the belt is missing to complete the scene which the "well-informed" visitor has pictured in his mind. Bam! a fist thunders onto the bar and its owner shouts into his neighbour's face that "she" was *so* an Italian. But the Italian doesn't want to have the lady-compatriot foisted on him and continues to insist that "she" was black. Passionately, the fight about the racial origin of the dark beauty continues in a slang of which I understand nothing, except the blow with the fist, with which the Italian finally puts a full stop after his oral argument. The opponent has the sharply pronounced features of the Russian Jew; but he is of unusually tall and strong build, and his slang and profanity would have made any Irishman envious. He hesitates for a moment and then a blow comes crashing down on the Italian skull. The noise of the drinking crowd has turned into a murmur, from which only the odd piercing cheer rises up. Already a circle has formed around the two opponents, the barkeeper jumps over the bar, not to make peace but to maintain order in the ring and to see to it that nobody interferes with this honest man-to-man fight. The two champions start thrashing at each other, the Italian, also a tall, strong fellow, more on the offensive. Suddenly he delivers a powerful punch to the other's belly, but the latter turns a little sideways and the menacing fist hits a whisky bottle in his rear coatpocket. Whichever may have aroused his indignation, the threat to his stomach or to his whisky, Juda the Lion is roused in him and, as if lashed by a savage hurricane, his fists descend left and right on the Italian. Already blood is squirting out of his mouth, he turns pale and swallows and seems ready to topple over — but then with a final crash, he throws himself onto the enemy. For a moment they wrestle, fall, roll around on the floor. Then the Italian is on the bottom, his eyes half-closed, utterly exhausted, but the other is kneeling on him, his muscles tensed and the ferocity of a tiger in his eyes. Is he going to slam his fist into the other's face once more? But already the barkeeper jumps in and yanks him up. "That's enough," he says, "he's down and out." As for me, though, I have to think of the maiden about whom the battle has raged. Is she really a purebred Italian, or is some of Ham's blood coursing in her veins? About one thing, certainly, there can be no doubt: she is a dangerous minx, this signorina!

It is not until the next morning when we go on that we see how beautifully the little town of Fernie nestles in the mountains. Three huge rocky peaks, "The Three Sisters," form the background. The forests all around the mountain slopes are, for the greater part, burnt out, and this bleak spectacle of charred trunks is with us off and on throughout the day. For a short time we continue on through mining country which gradually gives way to sawmills. Everywhere their lumbermen — having not much more sense than the fire itself — help it to complete its ravages. No one thinks of replanting the forest. In the afternoon we reach the southern point of the Kootenay Lake which stretches out over nearly 100 kilometres straight north, but midway sends an outflow westward, and from there, near the town of Nelson, issues the Kootenay River, which empties into the Columbia farther south. The Kootenay Lake, in proportion to its length a narrow strip of water, is closely surrounded by high timbered mountains. For hours there is no town, no settlement, no human being. But gradually, here and there, widely spaced, there begins to emerge a tiny area of cleared land, the field-brown square lined with green, a young orchard. Soil and climate are said to be excellently suited for fruit growing, the main difficulties being the costly clearing and the insufficient transportation facilities. These pioneers have made a strong impression on me, the way they settle in the middle of nowhere and plant little apple and plum trees in place of the immense old conifer forests, with nothing around for miles and miles but mountains, woods, and the lonely lake which sees hardly any traffic. As we come closer to Nelson, the small clearings become more frequent. But our attention has long since been diverted by a highly unusual phenomenon: the colours of sunset in the afternoon. The great disc is still standing high above our head, but smoke-tinged with a beautiful dark golden-yellow like the stove panelling in a farm house in Lower-Saxony. It sends reddish and violet vapours over the mountain forests on both sides, and its reflection flows in the water like liquid gold. "A small forest fire somewhere in the area," is the answer given with an indifferent shrug of the shoulders; and later, toward evening, we see thick trails of smoke coming out of one of the side valleys.

It went on like this during the next days of our trip: into Nelson, which nestles at the corner of the lake like a little upper-Italian city and picturesquely reaches up the riverside hills; on down the Kootenay, which speeds in merry leaps and bounds towards its estuary, dancing down the mighty Burlington Falls; on down the more dignified and slower Columbia River to Trail, where Canada's greatest smelters are located; and up the magnificent side valley at the end of which Rossland is situated with its gold mines; back again to the confluence of Kootenay and Columbia, and the third night and the third day northward along the two long Arrow Lakes. A greyish blue mist lay over all these valleys the whole time, sometimes very light and then again very thick, taking away the view of the more distant mountain ranges and frequently obscuring the crests of the nearest mountains, weaving softly like magic veils through the trees on both shores and playfully wrapping the afternoon sun in a bright-coloured haze of smoke. At times this is annoying to the traveller who is eager to see something, and then again it is so fascinatingly picturesque that the beautiful proximity makes him forget about the unknown distance ahead. But over all this hangs the bleak awareness — ever-present, depressing, disquieting — that somewhere up in the mountains or deep down in the valleys living, vigorously sprouting trees and forests are burning, charring. It is their mourning crape which envelops the entire country here. Sometimes the haze turns into dense smoke and everybody starts coughing even in the closed train compartment. Often it irritates one's eyes and nose, at least out on the rear platform; but frequently the smoke is too light even for that. What makes it so depressing, however, is this: day after day to pass by endlessly alternating stretches of live trees and stretches of charred trunks, day after day under the vapour and smoke of burning forests — sometimes the fire is far away, sometimes it is very close, but not once does it become visible. It is as if you heard through the wall of a room a sick man screaming with pain night after night and you couldn't go to him, and you couldn't help him even if permitted in; and yet, you sense his suffering all the more keenly because you are aware of it without seeing it.

Only later, on the Arrow Lake, did I have the occasion to see a forest fire. "A very small one," said the ship's officer who had already been observing it for three weeks. For the fire by now was in its last stages. Here and there a few trees were all ablaze, never more than two or three at the same time; like shining torches they reached up high into the black midnight. But all around, everything glimmered and smouldered. A rectangular area which burned stronger and rather brightly, a quarter of an acre perhaps, was the focal point of the entire picture. A horrifying and magnificent picture! Imagine the Heidelberg Castle in exotic yellow and red fireworks; imagine groups of students carrying shining, smoking torches at numerous points over the width and height of the mountain slope; imagine all the young people of the city, thousands of them, spread through the forest with sparkling, small, yellow and red lanterns. That is how British Columbia's forests burn in their third week! What a gay and colourful sacrificial feast for the God of Fire!

Despite the aesthetic and sentimental aspects of this sacrificial celebration, its material side should not be forgotten. Who offers up the sacrifice, and who bears the cost? The causes of the forest fires are numerous: camp fires which are not carefully extinguished; clearing fires which are not watched over; smaller sawmills that burn their wastes outside instead of using them up; train locomotives which let their sparks fly about; and discarded railway ties that are being thrown beside the tracks and burnt on site. This latter practice is, of course, strictly forbidden, not only by the authorities but also by the railway companies themselves. Not long ago, however, an official commission found that the practice is still quite common. The culprit here is almost exclusively the CPR and because this versatile and ubiquitous company, which is virtually God in western Canada, operates a regular newsbureau together with its telegraph system, it can easily keep such unpleasant facts at least out of its own press. Underlying all the individual reasons for the forest fires, however, there is the one general causative factor — the great dryness which is usual in the late summer months. A few sparks can create the greatest havoc then. Once the fire has broken out and is spreading, almost no human hand can extinguish it. Often it is impossible even to push it back and contain it. The only effective weapons against forest fires are strict rules for their prevention. Unflagging vigilance on the part of the government fire-lookouts can do a lot, but not everything. The number of these lookouts has been greatly increased since last year and, indeed, the forest fires have done considerably less damage. Knowledgeable and reliable observers are, however, of the opinion that the measures taken by the government are still completely inadequate, and they view the future of British Columbia's forests with some concern.

The totally innocent victims of the destruction of the forests will be the farmers. Already the all-important problem for them is how to obtain enough water. The barer the mountain slopes get through fire and greediness, the more difficult and pressing the problem becomes. So far the devastation is confined mainly to the small southern corner of the province, the only part settled so far, perhaps a tenth of a total area which is as big as Germany, Holland, Belgium, Switzerland, and Italy combined. For the wood industry it is comfort enough that they will be able to fall back on the forest regions in the North when the southern corner is exhausted and burnt out. But what good will the forests up there be to the farmer if the sources of productivity and prosperity dry up down here? That is a question which concerns not only the fruit growers who are beginning to settle in British Columbia's mountain valleys. Almost the entire agriculture of the southern prairie provinces depends on the precipitation which, at least partly, depends on the forestry resources of the mountains. It seems as though not even the farmers of British Columbia, any more than the farmers of the rest of western Canada, treat the matter of forest fires and forest depletion as seriously as it deserves to be treated.

Shortly before the Columbia River crosses into American territory a narrow side valley reaches it from the west, dropping down sharply from the mountains, framed on both sides by magnificent forests. For the fire has not yet extended its bony claws this far. But how long will this peace last? For even now, throughout the day, a light haze of smoke obscures the sun and shrouds the more distant mountain peaks. The higher our little train wheezes up the valley, the more frequently vegetable and fruit farms rather than forests reach up into the mountain. At last the valley opens into a wide, fertile, green, ever-rising basin from which the little town of Rossland, halfway up the hillside, smiles down picturesquely. How different such a mining town in British Columbia is in its total outlook on life, its spiritual make-up, its collective awareness, from the settlement centres of the wheat-growing prairie provinces! Unlike them it is not a product or a function of its surroundings, but centres in itself. There the old saying still applies: "If the farmer prospers, everybody prospers." Nothing occupies the mind of the city-dweller more than how the farmers' crops are turning out, what progress agriculture has been making, and what prospects lie ahead of it. In British Columbia the farmer seems, so far at least, to be an appendage of the city; he usually settles only in its vicinity because he considers himself to be dependent on its market. The people in these mountain communities, not only in Rossland, seem calmer, focusing more on themselves than the people under the free winds of the prairie; they seem less affected by the world outside, and less interested in drawing it closer to themselves.

Rossland is different for yet another reason. To all these places in the Northwest the word Past is unknown; even the Present means nothing to them, the Future is everything. Rossland is not an older town either, being not even two decades old, and yet its yesterday was greater than its today. In the mid-Nineties it experienced an enormous boom. Rich ore deposits were discovered, and the gold fever rose to the highest pitch; in a short time the first little mining camp became a city of 8,000. Today we find a stately place with many solid buildings, but here and there also quite a number of abandoned and dilapidated little houses. The population is said to be 4,000 at the present time, but this estimate is probably still too high. The exaggerated expectations have come down somewhat in the meantime. At any rate, there appears to be enough ore to support a good-sized mining town. Between 1905 and 1908 the average output was approximately 3.4 million dollars. This year, however, only one pit is working to full capacity, the "Centre Star" and "War Eagle," which are technically and economically one unit and belong to the Consolidated Mining and Smelting Company of Canada. By the way, one of the owners of this nice long name is again the CPR. The five other pits of consequence in Rossland were shut down last March — temporarily shut down was the immediate report. The worked veins had become scarce, but new ore was expected to be found soon. In the meantime, at the beginning of September, the Le Roi Mine was opened again, so far only with 80 men. In Rossland it is widely believed that speculative manoeuvres were the real reason for the shutdown. Be that as it may, the population of this little town has suffered severely.

"You must take one of these apples as a souvenir," said the fruit-grower in the Rossland Valley as he showed me his most beautiful apple tree. Later in the afternoon, when the affable superintendent of the Centre Star Mine showed me around in the underground tunnels, I expected a similar invitation: "Wouldn't you like to break off a little piece of this gold ore?" . . . When descending a gold mine for the first time, one doesn't exactly expect to find gold nuggets on the walls, but one does anticipate seeing at least little specks of gold scattered here and there through the rock. Oh, what disappointment! There is nothing to be seen but rock and more rock, and in several spots there is a glint of iron ore. But the people here are not at all interested in iron, they are looking for more precious things. Gold, copper, and silver are hidden in their iron ore — so well hidden, in fact, that not even the most thorough crushing reveals anything; only smelting furnaces and electrolysis extract enough of the precious metals to make them visible and profitable. Two tons of ore must be mined in order to obtain, after all these lengthy processes, one ounce of gold. True, these same two tons of ore also contain twenty pounds of copper and a trace of silver, but the silver is of no importance at all and the total amount of copper is only worth about one-sixth of the one grain of gold. It is the gold that lures and draws the men, four hundred of them, into the dark depths of this mountain day after day. They have dug themselves 760 metres below the surface. The tunnels, if laid end to end, would extend from here, so close to the Pacific, all the way to the Atlantic Ocean, 4,000 kilometres away. What they found was rock and rock again, and a grey mineral ore. Who would not be enticed by the red metal when it shines up through the water, just as Alberich [in the Nibelungen Saga] gathers it from the Rhine River, or the Klondikers, in more modest quantities, from the Yukon. Of the gold miners in Rossland not one, however, has seen with his own eyes even a glimmer of the gold which he extracts from the bowels of the earth!

Whether or not Rossland's other mines are nearing the depletion stage, nobody in the Centre Star or War Eagle is afraid of meeting with such a fate. The mine superintendent assures me that the presently available deposits alone could still be mined another ten years with the same intensity and productivity. However, new deposits are found constantly. Only last year a seam was discovered on the sixth level at a depth of 260 metres which is richer than all the others worked so far. The narrow passage through which we are walking opens up to the size of a larger room. "This is the new working pit," my guide explains. "In the first year we took gold worth one million dollars from this room."

That the present fades in comparison with the so recent past is rather hard on the remaining inhabitants. But the people do not complain, they don't even discuss it. They toss their heads back and say: "Our future will be better than the past ever was!" The land that has sustained Rossland up to now will continue to do so. But as the past and the present lived off the inorganic treasures of the land, so the future should develop its organic potential. Great things are expected from fruit-farming in this area. The soil appears to be extremely fertile and the climate is mild enough even in winter despite the considerable elevation. Already there are a number of prospering fruit farms, although the general attention is only now beginning to turn to this intensive soil cultivation. Apples, plums, pears, and all sorts of berries are the main produce. For the first time I came across the wonderberry, developed by Luther Burbank from two inedible fruits: the African stubbleberry *(Solanum guineense)* and the West-American "rabbit plant" *(Solanum villosum)*. Like a large seaweed the grey-greenish plant spreads close to the ground in a circle of approximately 50 centimetres in diameter. The berries, of which many plants grow more than one hundred, look like huckleberries but have a very subtle and sweet taste, almost like grapes. They are likely to become popular quickly, especially as marmalade.

The farms in British Columbia are, of course, quite a bit smaller than those in the prairie provinces, partly because the arable land is limited, partly because the intensive fruit and vegetable cultivation, which is made possible and encouraged by the soil and climate, requires capital and a lot of individual labour. Most of the farms are ten acres in size, and the cost per acre is at least $120. The most difficult time for the fruit farmer is the first five or six years, until the trees actually begin to produce. In the meantime he has to grow vegetables or small fruit in order to come through somehow. At times he might work in the mine or for the railways. Besides, as a rule the land is bought on a ten-year instalment plan. Despite all this it is considered impossible to start out with less than $1,500, even if one doesn't want to live better than the prairie farmer who takes up a homestead with a capital of $300. However, once the trees actually start to bear fruit, the fruit-grower is richly repaid. People everywhere can name cases where the costs of land and operating capital were recovered in one stroke in the first actual year of production. It is the layman's impression, at any rate, that the yields in the entire province of British Columbia are substantially larger than those in Germany. It is just a delight to see these trees; often the eye cannot make out the green leaves for the red of the apples or the more subdued colour of the peach. The individual fruits, too, are usually much bigger and more beautiful than ours. One hardly ever sees fruit of medium or poor quality. Yet it seems to me that the best sorts of our fruit are somewhat more aromatic than the ones here. Possibly this is a consequence of the artificial irrigation which is predominantly used here. The fact that irrigated sugar beets produce greater quantities but have less sugar content than the non-irrigated ones would suggest this. However, I couldn't find one expert here who would confirm my theory, for no Canadian is objective enough to admit the superior aroma of any kind of foreign fruit.

Farther up north, around the two long stretched-out Arrow Lakes, fruit growing will find a larger area than in the Rossland Valley. Settlement in this area is also still in its infancy, scarcely more than two years old. In Nakusp on the Upper Arrow Lake, however, there is one farm which has already been in operation for 12 years. Oddly enough it belongs to a Chinese man who recognized the natural destiny of this area one decade before the white owners of the land. For a long time the white men had crossed these lakes, but they did not recognize the fertility of the soil or the mildness of the climate. Their eyes sought the red metal, for they were miners and prospectors — gold, gold, gold was their sole desire. How often has not this spectacle repeated itself in the course of history: gold and precious stones lure man to discover and colonize new lands. Only after generations does he realize that the new countries have much better things to give than gold and gems. He is forever thinking of the inorganic treasures of the earth, and it is always the organic ones that really enrich him in the end. What has the western hemisphere given to mankind? Wheat, maize, cotton, beef cattle, and shoe-leather, etc.: these are more valuable than all its precious metals combined. But how pallid and commonplace would such a promise have sounded to the Spanish and Portuguese seafarers and conquistadores; they would never have followed it to conquer the New World! Perhaps our descendants will say similar things about us when at some time in the future Southwest Africa exports beef cattle and our tropical colonies supply the mother-country with cotton: first a few diamonds had to be found so that Germany's capital would discover its own colonies! That is how it happened and how it is still happening in British Columbia. A great number of white settlers now are following the lone Chinese pioneer. Yet, while the Asian grows vegetables almost exclusively, the White Man looks for better earnings in fruit growing. I was frequently told that the Chinese were no fruit growers at all, but that they had no equal in vegetable farming.

All the arable land here in the Columbia valley, part of which is the area of the Arrow Lakes, including the land in the Kootenay valley, belonged to the CPR and for the most part still does. They got it as a subsidy for building railways in the interior of the province. In all, the Company in British Columbia received approximately two million hectares, of which 218,000 have been sold so far. But out here the Company seems to have much less interest in colonization and in healthy agricultural development than it has in the prairie provinces.

From the northern point of the Upper Arrow Lake a short railway line runs to the CPR mainline in Revelstoke, which then takes the traveller in one day's ride to the shore of the Pacific Ocean—to Vancouver. Not far beyond Revelstoke I made a side-trip to the south into the Okanagan Valley, one of the older fruit-growing areas called "the garden of British Columbia." This year, I was told, has been a bad one — frost in spring and persistent dryness throughout the summer. The yield is said to be poorer than usual, but for a stranger it still is impressive enough. A lovely wide valley with beautiful side-valleys. The Okanagan Lake, 150 kilometres long, fills two-thirds of the main valley; they say that the most beautiful fruit is grown on its shores. A place like Peachland, "the land of peaches" — the mere name makes your mouth water just reading the train schedule. But when you discover on Saturday that according to the schedule all wheels, those of the train and of the paddle steamer, stand still on Sundays, then you must suppress your appetite for the "juicy" little village. I had to be satisfied with visiting Vernon, the biggest town in the Okanagan Valley, and the nearby renowned fruit farm of Lord Aberdeen, the former Governor General of Canada. Seventeen years ago, when Lord Aberdeen was buying land here, there were already white people in the area — a few ranch-owners and cowboys. The land was only used for cattle-raising on large ranches. Gradually farmers, too, came into the valley. The ranches were more and more divided up and put to the plough. Thus agriculture and mixed farming took the place of mere ranching. During this entire period the Aberdeen farm in Coldstream was engaged in fruit production, and the number of imitators increased steadily. Just as in the past the ranches were divided up into farms, so now the farms, from 64 to 200 hectares in size, are being divided up into fruit farms of from four to ten hectares. For several years now fruit-growing has been in first place. Agriculture and dairy farming have not disappeared entirely, but they have definitely become secondary operations.

In the English squire tradition, Lord Aberdeen, who owns a second estate farther up on the Okanagan Lake, of course has never operated his farms himself. That was perhaps a good thing, for the man who has been running Coldstream for 14 years has made it well known as a model farm throughout Canada and nobody knows whether His Lordship personally would have achieved such a success himself. The manager of Coldstream also belongs to an aristocracy, maybe to a nobler one than the Very Honourable Earl of Aberdeen, namely to the high nobility of classical, political economy; his grandfather was David Ricardo [the English economist]. Whether the genius of theoretical political economics is normally hereditary, that it should bring forth a practical agriculturist of great talent in the third generation, may be open to question. But perhaps his grandfather's talent can be found again in an achievement by Mr. W. C. Ricardo which in itself alone would be of very little consequence. Anyone travelling through Canada who has a certain interest in economic matters can barely escape from all the advertising brochures and pamphlets with which he is bombarded from all sides in the most amiable manner. The main purpose of this literature is to attract settlers; and between the authorities of the various provinces, the communities, and the Boards of Trade, there is a veritable contest going on in propagating such publications. The Dominion Government advertises equally for the whole country with its own brochures, and finally there are entire promotion libraries which are being put out by the railway companies, the real estate firms, and similar interested parties. As long as these brochures supply facts they are valuable advisers to the travellers. However, most of them bury their factual information in a mush of verbosity and bombastic exaggeration which after a certain time become either unpalatable or comical. Thus it is a pleasure to receive the prospectus of the Coldstream farm in the Okanagan Valley which gives all pertinent information with concise and clear matter-of-factness as becomes a Mr. Ricardo.

A still greater pleasure is a visit to the Coldstream farm itself. There we find entire fields of orchards which look immense; and if the trunks are not as tall as we are used to seeing them, their splendid crowns, for all that, are so laden and colourful with ripe fruit that it makes your eyes light up just to walk between the rows. The greater part of the harvest is already in, and with great pride they show me through a storage building that contains, from right to left, from the bottom almost to the ceiling, nothing but big and small, green, yellow, and red apples. For apples are the main fruit here; plums, pears, and cherries are not totally neglected, but a large-scale operation does not like to bother with small fruit. Today the fruit trees alone already cover an area of 160 hectares, and that is continually enlarged. In addition, hops play an important role — 44 hectares are reserved for them. Grain crops and cattle-raising are considered to be secondary, whereas the farm's poultry, presently 2,000 birds, is well-known throughout British Columbia. Coldstream presently has a size of 5,200 hectares, a little more than half of which is mountain land and of value only as a property asset. Of the other 2,400 hectares, one half is to remain permanently under the farm's administration. The second half is going to be divided up and gradually sold in small parcels of ten to twenty acres for $200 to $250 per acre. That is not cheap, especially since the cost of irrigation, which is indispensable for fruit-growing here, must be added. A large irrigation enterprise is connected with the Coldstream farm, which, once it is entirely completed, will supply 8,000 hectares with water. The fruit-growers who settle here are almost exclusively Englishmen, some of them retired officers, former officials, and people of similar middle-class background for whom the term "farmer" would be ill-suited. Besides, their main objective is not the greatest possible acquisition of money. They want to spend their days in a pleasant climate, with work that is agreeable and not too hard, and at the same time they want a comfortable return for their small capital investment. The Coldstream farm accommodates its buyers and settlers by relieving them, for a moderate fee, if they wish, of the initial tedious soil cultivation, the planting and waiting during the first few years, because in no occupation is the beginning more difficult and more demanding of patience than in fruit-growing. For its own needs and those of the settlers, Coldstream also operates a tree nursery which covers more than 12 hectares.

The living quarters of these settlers are not farm houses; they are English cottages, simple and pretty, with many long rows of apple trees on both sides, small fruit plots and narrow vegetable fields in between. Everything blends into a picture of such a well-ordered civilized region that one forgets one is in the New — almost in the Newest — World. But then there is again a huge hop-field of the Coldstream farm which quickly reminds one of reality. Groups of red-brown men are spread out all over it, occupied with pulling down the green festoons, and on the ground sit the red-brown women with their broadfaced and blackhaired children, picking and gathering the green lumps on large sheets of burlap. Two hundred Indian families are at work. Their rust-coloured skin and the red dresses of the women go peculiarly well with the intense green of the hops, and give the field a colourful and animated appearance. I walk a few rows in and start a conversation which only stumbles on with difficulty. For the people's knowledge of English appears to be far less perfect in reality than in our beautifully stylized Indian stories. Among other things, I try to explain that I am a foreigner. From G e r m a n y. But the word doesn't seem to ring a bell, it is obviously completely unknown. Then, when I have a closer look at the picked hops, an old Indian says: "You understand hops?" — "No," I confess frankly; "or only when it is combined with malt and is drinkable." As I make an emphatic drinking gesture he gets the message and grins with delight. But all of a sudden he becomes absolutely stonefaced and serious. One can see a thought combination forming behind his square forehead, and then he exclaims, almost lively, and with a grin from ear to ear: "Oh, G e r m a n! . . . G e r m a n! . . ." And with a repeated drinking gesture and unchanging grin he tries to make the women on the ground also understand that I am a German, a member of the beer-drinking nation. My patriotic feeling, which had been not a little wounded by the Indians' initial ignorance of the German name, proudly recovers. Truly, all is not yet lost for our nation! As long as the noble art of beer-brewing and the still nobler art of beer-drinking are not yet lost on pale faces and redskins alike, Germany's name and fame shall not perish!

Vancouver and Victoria — the two extreme outposts of the British world power, the extreme outposts of English culture. No, they are more! If anywhere there should exist that great wall of our fairy tales where the world ends, then it is here. This coast line is the last frontier, not only of the Western Hemisphere, but of our entire European-American sphere of power and culture. The Great Ocean is the great world divide. When the fiery sun with its mysterious violet veils sinks into it from the sky, then we feel that we are witnessing the final, the true sunset. For the first time the East is not in our backs but beyond the setting sun. Here our world ends and there a new one begins: the "Land of the Rising Sun," the world of the Mongol race!

For the foreigner who stands on this western edge for the first time, this experience is a revelation. Those living here sense the world divide no less strongly. But for them it is not a poetic, mystery-laden beauty but a quite real factor in their daily public and private lives. The people consider themselves constantly on outpost duty: outpost of the white race against the yellow, outpost of Greater Britannia at the western wing of the Empire, outpost of the good English middle-class against the parvenu civilization of young America.

This awareness of being on outpost duty gives the people a certain tautness and concentration. They feel responsible. The self-satisfied egotism which characterizes the pioneer of the interior of western Canada has disappeared. For the inhabitants of the endless prairie, all foreign countries are a world away. They laugh in a good-natured superior way when the newspapers report on fleet controversies and war-cries in far-away London. Here on the Pacific Coast, the questions of world politics are taken very seriously, not only the questions which affect one personally and on which one has an opinion, such as the relationship with Japan. The German-English question, too, is being discussed with lively interest in Vancouver and Victoria, perhaps not in the same way as in London, but the same as in Manchester or Glasgow. "Will there really be a war?" the German visitor is asked and his treatment, in great contrast to that received in the interior of western Canada, reveals a slightly embarrassed politeness with the undertone, "We are gentlemen and won't hold this against you personally."

English outposts — that is the first impression. And it is retained in Victoria, the capital and official residence of the Lieutenant Governor. In the trade and harbour city of Vancouver it might be blurred somewhat during the next few days. About half of Vancouver is Americanized. Vancouver works feverishly, makes money feverishly, expands feverishly — all specifically American activities. The inhabitants themselves are not quite sure whether to be prouder of the American or the English element in their city, of their American business life or their English private life.

Speaking first of external impressions, perhaps the hustle and bustle in the streets is American, but Vancouver's street picture as a whole is totally different from that of its rivals in the United States. The business houses are not always beautiful, but they have a certain uniform character, and a number of banking houses reflecting more than ordinary taste adorn the whole without being over-bearing. Even in the typical American city they do not only build according to material considerations, yet the occasional aesthetic efforts are as a rule boringly uninspired imitations and usually stand out from the total picture naively and persistently. Above all, the people in every corner of the United States must have their sky-scraper — often squeezed in between wooden shacks — and then they feel almost equal to the universally envied metropolis of New York. The city of millions on the narrow Manhattan Island was forced to build upwards because the Hudson and East River left it no room on either side. Out in the country such business towers don't make sense; they are in any case not a consequence of high land prices but often their cause. That Vancouver has been more successful in steering clear of this absurd tastelessness than Winnipeg, for instance, is proof of its better English culture.

How misused are the terms "culture" and "civilization"! Nowhere, however, does their true meaning become clearer and nowhere is it more inevitable to talk about them than on a trip from the U.S. into Canada. I find the individual American as a rule more congenial and more likable than the individual Englishman or English-Canadian. But, multiplied by 100, by 1,000, by a million, John Bull suddenly seems much closer to me than Uncle Sam does. Others who are in a position to make valid comparisons appear to have this same experience: that we Germans at first feel more at home in Canada than in the U.S. We may like the Americans personally better, but they belong to another social stratum within the society of nations. That harmony between outer and inner civilization that constitutes culture seems to give to the old countries of Europe, perhaps to all old countries, a feeling of community as against the New World. After a prolonged stay in the United States, a well-known Japanese personality once admitted to me: "I long to live again in a country of old culture, in Japan or in Germany." — It wasn't meant as a slight against America: it was an involuntary sigh from the heart. How many Americans would understand this? Culture is a magic cloak which only those who wear it around their own shoulders seem to be able to see. The most luxurious hotels, the most comfortable sleeping cars, the most expensive paintings — and even the most expensive women — are signs of the most highly developed civilization, but they have nothing whatsoever to do with culture.

Are you asking me to prove Vancouver's superior culture to you? The visitor in a hurry senses it instinctively. Later on he looks for objective arguments. But naturally there are more illustrations than there is evidence. For this precisely is the difference between civilization and culture: the one can be assessed in dollars and cents, but the other cannot. In case the houses haven't convinced you yet, look at the people in the street, especially at the women, because they reflect countries and cities more faithfully than the male population. Perhaps this is so because the women are the stable portion of the population. The strangers in the city are mostly men, and the men of the city travel more to other places — a fact that tends to obscure the national and local character. The ladies do not enliven Vancouver's street scene as entertainingly as they do in the United States. They are dressed much more simply and, although this in itself is not a shortcoming, quite a pretty sparkle is lost to which the eye has become accustomed in the New World. But how much awkwardness is avoided at the same time! All that American slavery to fashion, the extent of which one outside of the country can scarcely imagine. Just as every little one-horse town has to adopt New York's sky-scraper, so every little shop-girl has to follow the latest New York style. The elegant fashion designed with precious and beautiful material in mind becomes a travesty when copied in a threadbare and cheap fabric. Nevertheless I am not saying the English simplicity of Vancouver's fair sex is more gratifying on the whole. It is, however, evidence of good breeding, and if not of a well-developed sense of beauty then at least of a well-developed sense of tact.

In the appearance of Vancouver's men the predominance of the English traits cannot be overlooked, either. It is evident in the slimmer physique, in the narrower face, in the English-style moustache, in the better manners and lesser cordiality and candour, in the better fabrics of the clothing because America with its high custom duties has to adulterate its so-called woollens with poor cotton material. However, that is only the private side. The business activity of these same people has a wholly American character. Vancouver was founded as the terminal point of the CPR in 1885. Twenty years later it had a population of 45,000, and today it can be estimated at around 85,000 as the authorities give a figure of 100,000. The significance of the city still lies in the fact that it is the junction between Canada's only Transcontinental Railway and the ocean traffic to Asia, Australia, Alaska, as well as to the more southerly regions of the American continent. There is also regular shipping traffic to Europe, in which a strong increase is expected after completion of the Panama Canal.

Vancouver is situated on a peninsula between two elongated and spacious ocean bays. The northern one, Burrard Inlet, of immense size and deep enough for the hugest ocean liners, forms the city's harbour. A high mountain range gives protection against the northern winds, and the narrows offer an almost too cautious access from the sea. However, the government is in the process of removing any doubt as to the safety and comfort of the passage by investing one million dollars in this project. In the course of the next few years, the very flat rear part of the ocean inlet, called False Creek, is going to be filled in. The front part, English Bay, lies wide open and exposed to the inclemency of the weather. Real estate people plan to build another harbour here. This is technically quite feasible if a very costly pier is erected. The economic benefit, however, is highly dubious, to put it mildly, and I only mention this project because they intend to seek the capital for its construction from Germany this year. Vancouver's natural harbour, Burrard Inlet, has still a huge unused shoreline and the various experts assure me that it would suffice for many decades, even with the most rapid development.

That a still greater economic growth than the one experienced so far lies ahead for the city of Vancouver is probably not an overly rash prophecy. Apart from the CPR, the hill railways — The Great Northern and The Northern Pacific — already pass through Vancouver, and in the coming decade the city will also become the Pacific terminal of the Canadian Northern, which is going to be built from Edmonton, Alberta, through the Yellow Head Pass and then, presumably, through the valley of the Northern Thompson River to the southwest. In British Columbia's North, the Grand Trunk Pacific is constructing a new harbour city, Prince Rupert, where their main line is supposed to reach the Ocean by a fairly straight route from Edmonton. In Vancouver, they don't seem to be overly worried by the prospect of competition. Indeed, two cities on Canada's Pacific shore are not too many. Incidentally, Vancouver, today — as she will for many years to come — profits from the construction and food provision for the future rival. The Grand Trunk Pacific also plans to build a branch line from the Yellow Head Pass through the Fraser Valley to Vancouver later on, so that the city would then have five different railway lines.

In decades to come, an increasing portion of western Canada's natural products, especially Alberta's rapidly increasing output, will certainly be shipped from the Pacific Ocean. For it is only half as far (644 miles) from Calgary to Vancouver as from Calgary to Fort William, where today the entire export of the Canadian prairie is to be transported via the Great Lakes. So far the CPR has been taking advantage of its transcontinental monopoly with American ruthlessness and has been insisting, just because of the double distance, on shipping everything to the East. Furthermore, the Great Lakes freeze up in mid-December. Then the entire distance to the Atlantic must be covered by rail, which again involves the CPR. For the farmer this means great losses; every year, on the 12th of December, the price of wheat in Winnipeg automatically falls by five cents per bushel. The entire crop cannot possibly be shipped before that time. Besides, the farmers are getting more and more into the habit of holding back their wheat in view of the market fluctuations (although such practices were long ago denounced and condemned as "wheat usury" by the Psalmist and the Church Fathers Ambrosius and Basilius). You see, the people on the prairie are becoming more and more godless and, slowly but surely, just as calculating as the city dwellers. Therefore the farmers are just waiting until, in five or six years' time, the monopoly of the CPR will be broken, and then they are going to ship a large part of their wheat and cattle via the permanently ice-free Pacific route.

Vancouver would be all too un-American if long ago it hadn't duly—or perhaps sometimes even unduly—taken into account this great future development. Land speculation is in full blossom as it is in all these western places. Naturally, poisonous blossoms are no rarity. It doesn't necessarily always have to be a fraudulent scheme like the one in which a few real estate agents purchased a strip of land on the Pacific Coast, divided it into building lots and named the town they were about to found Prince Rupert. Then they looked for buyers by advertising on a grand scale, pretending it was the new city of Prince Rupert where the Grand Trunk Pacific would reach the Ocean. This rankest swindle was noised abroad so blatantly that, after some time, the Board of Trade put an end to the activity. In general one should always keep in mind that in a young colonial country such as this, dubious and even less clumsy manoeuvres can in no way be avoided. Therefore one must strongly condemn the attempt to lure European capital into land speculation out here. Unfortunately, one must also warn against Germans who act as decoys for such activities.

All around Vancouver's harbour there are also more pleasant things than land speculation. To the north, opposite the city, the first slopes and peaks of the Canadian Coastal Mountains rise almost directly out of the blue ripples of the Burrard Inlet to a height of 1,000 to 2,000 metres. Where the foot of the mountain range recedes a little, the stately suburb of North

Vancouver tries to make use of the free space. Near the bay which opens into the Georgia Strait and the Pacific, the buildings of an old Indian mission paint a few milky-white dots into the landscape. Above it, however, lusciously dense dark forests cover the backs of the mountains and over their shoulders, from some range farther back, two crooked and naked rocky peaks beckon invitingly to the admiring visitor. The most beautiful side of the Burrard Inlet is its western end. Here the peninsula on which Vancouver is situated widens toward the north, and between the bay and the open water lies the most magnificent park that a city anywhere could pride itself on possessing. But no! This Stanley Park is not a park, nor has it been laid out. It is a virgin forest which has been left standing! A well-cared-for road runs around it, always along the water, and a number of paths are cut through, but one step off the path to the right or to the left leads into the wildest brush, or actually over it, for anyone who does not cut a trail with his axe like the first discoverers and pioneers will have to perform a merry climbing feat. The characteristic of the virgin forest is not so much the upright healthy trees which have grown to an overwhelming height in their long lives, as those which have been felled by age or decay, by the voracity of parasites, or by the lightning from above. Now they lie about in a wild jumble, for years and decades, continue to rot and give nourishment to the densest exotic shrubs and brush, elder bushes and lianas, which spread their mesh among dead and living trunks, ruthlessly advancing, strangling each other, unruly, almost impenetrable. Decay and warmth and humidity of the coastal climate cover the ground with a high soft cushion of all kinds of moss and ferns. But far above them, giant spruce trunks tower high into the winds, fifty, seventy, eighty, the boldest up to one hundred metres high. There they stand with their immense girth of 10 to 15 metres — and yet magnificently lithe when we bend our heads far, far backwards to let our eyes climb up to their tops. Firmly rooted, defiant and proud, they hold together this primeval thicket which spreads over 1,500 acres. Jungles in tropical lands may perhaps evoke all the profuse fantasies of *1001 Nights,* but this home-like, nordic virgin forest leads us back into the old familiar fairy tales. And as the last rays of the sun steal through this dense and stubborn tangle, Sleeping Beauty's golden locks shine forth out of the blue-black dusk, and somewhere there in the distance the Prince's silver helmet glints and glistens. . . .

By the time I have worked my way out of the forest onto the wide road right next to the rocky seashore, the sun has already disappeared far back into the Pacific. For the first time the blue mountain range of Vancouver Island that stretches out in front of it emerges out of the mist before my eyes. Already all thoughts of things German have faded away and, as the outline of the slopes in the west and the coastal mountains in the north become less distinct, as the sky is painted in brilliant and yet so strangely subtle hues, the little clouds behind the Georgia Strait appear like gold-tinged green silk and lilac lace, and here and there from the darkening waters the white caps peep curiously — one's eyes, after having gazed long and restlessly westward, look inward: where have they seen this fairy-like fine interplay of evening hues before? . . . In the landscapes of Japanese artists! There is the same unique harmony of strength and gentleness in the silhouette of their mountains and in the peculiar colours of the entire picture. I have never been to Japan and don't know whether the east and west shores of the Pacific Ocean really possess this particular similarity — the same air and the same humidity. So far I have never seen an American or Canadian piece of art which actually showed these wonders and beauty. Is it perhaps that the Japanese who, they say, will yet fight with Anglo-Saxons for economic and political domination of the Pacific, have already conquered the Great Ocean in their art?

* * *

Victoria! The city is not only called so, it veritably shouts it into one's face. When we left Vancouver at noon, the city and the coastal mountains lay under the usual cloud cover, chilly rain chased most of the visitors below deck, and the wind whistled a tune to the dance of the little waves. However, after we had crossed the Georgia Straight, and our route had led around the southeast part of Vancouver Island through forest-fringed channels, the sun pulled the grey curtain back with increasing frequency and for longer intervals, and although it had already set when we turned into the Strait of Juan de Fuca, we felt as though, between noon and evening, we had come into another and milder clime. As we enter the beautiful bay harbour, the city appears to welcome us: Victoria! it calls out in a gay sunny clear voice. It is pleased with its life, it is pleased with itself; but of course it expresses this pleasure with the cool, quiet reserve of the English temperament.

"It is fall," the people sigh in near-by Vancouver. The calendar has almost reached October and, as far as the conditions of the Western Hemisphere are concerned, we are quite far north here. When thinking of Victoria, however, one can only think of spring, so friendly and mild does the breeze blow here; and they say it blows like that throughout the year. Winter is short and not cold, summer is longer and not hot. Clouds, rain, and fog are less frequent than on the continental coast. All the gardens are still in full bloom and sweet-smelling, and girls with smiling blue eyes pick roses on Christmas Day. Flowers, lawns, gardens around every house are the landmarks of Victoria, and on clear days the snowy range of the Olympic Mountains appears beyond the Strait of Juan de Fuca like a sublime accompaniment to the lovely spring melody of this little city.

I saw nothing more un-American in Canada than this place: life's harbour for superannuated English officers and employees. But Victoria is not inactive. Focal point for the development of Vancouver Island and market place for the developed regions; port of call for the traffic to Asia and Australia. Furthermore it is the seat of British Columbia's provincial government. But the most characteristic and extremely peculiar thing in the New World remains this class of people who live on annuities and pensions. A completely English town. English culture in the clean little houses, in the gardens, in the few public buildings, in the shops and in the window displays. English trends of thought. "Does Germany actually *have* to conquer *our* colonies?" an employee of the conservative provincial government asks me emphatically and in all earnestness.

Perhaps these thoughts suggest themselves so easily because not far away is Esquimalt, former naval port and military base of the British fleet in the Pacific. For years the Japanese Pact has made possible the concentration of the entire war fleet in England's native waters. Since then, Esquimalt has been lying idle and orphaned. A magnificent large and safe port. The dry-dock and all the buildings of the marine administration, probably also the fortifications, are kept in good condition. Only the little wooden houses of the civilians who, of course, for the most part have moved away, convey a sadly deserted and dilapidated impression. And yet, here and there a house is already being repaired, and people with the strong red faces of seamen and inn-keepers are taking a look at another one — what is going on here? The newspapers have reported that the Canadian government is planning to use the harbour for its own future colonial fleet. The report seems to be confirmed and seems to awaken Esquimalt to new life.

[The author's narrative ends abruptly here.]

EPILOGUE — A SON'S REFLECTIONS

Wilhelm Cohnstaedt was not unlike the virtuous travellers described by Edward Gibbon, the author of *The Decline and Fall of the Roman Empire*. Like them, he had that "virtue which borders on a vice, the flexible temper which can assimilate itself to every tone of society from the court to the cottage; the happy flow of spirits which can amuse and be amused in every company and situation."

This temper and quality of empathy with people he met was matched by an astute understanding which selected for observation and interpretation many issues and objects that are still significant over half a century later. James M. Minifie comments (in his *Homesteader: The Prairie Boyhood Recalled*) on those factors hidden in the future when his father had to make decisions which would be controlling not only for his own life, but for the lives of his descendents.

My father Wilhelm Cohnstaedt was 28 years old when, in 1909, he wrote this series of reports on the four western Canadian provinces. Written informally as "letters to one's neighbours back home," they offer a wealth of social and economic impressions concerning the rapidly developing culture of the pioneers settling western Canada early in this century. With his boundless curiosity and his extraordinary skill in selecting detail, the writer presents his vivid, interesting and surprisingly accurate generalizations — timely both then and now — about the unfolding economy and community life he observed in his travels through Manitoba, Saskatchewan, Alberta, and British Columbia.

He was born into a Jewish middle-class family in Frankfort on the Main, Germany, in 1880. His father, Ludwig Cohnstaedt, founded the "Handelsblatt," the economic and financial section of the *Frankfurter Zeitung* daily newspaper. Ludwig became acknowledged as the father of independent German economic and financial journalism. From this stimulating family background, Wilhelm Cohnstaedt learned to love the use of the written language and the power of critical journalism. He became (in 1907) the New York foreign correspondent for the *Frankfurter Zeitung* after completing his university studies and military service. In the summer and fall of 1909, before leaving America, he made his western Canadian tour and wrote the articles printed here.

In his formative years, Wilhelm Cohnstaedt had been surrounded with the challenges of a newly-industrialized Germany and with an intellectual spirit that blossomed in a country searching for a new identity of nationhood. He had an extensive university background in economics and history, having completed his Ph.D. degree at the University of Munich under Lujo Brentano. The fact that his thesis was on the agricultural policy of the German Social Democratic Party helps to explain the interest in — and insight into — land use and food production evident in these reports which he sent to the *Frankfurter Zeitung* from western Canada.

When my father was a student, Germany's universities were producing disciplined methodologists and inspired thinkers. Nothing was too sacred for critical examination: capitalism, religion, medicine, or land use. His university experience strengthened a commitment to a belief that knowledge contributes to the advancement of one's personal interests and those of society.

Substantial preparation guided his travel observations. His was not the fleeting interest of a tourist but the steadier perspective of a man informed about his readers' interests.

He was greatly influenced by Germany's intellectual giant of that time (and later his friend), Max Weber, as well as by the agricultural economist, Max Sering. Like Weber and Sering, he believed that the most efficient use of land was through independent family farm units, and that political stability could be achieved only through a permanently settled, self-determining population. He admired the prairie settlement patterns as contrasted with those of eastern Europe, where large estates were commonly run by the landed gentry and farmed by tenants or migrant labourers.

In his preoccupation with ethnic settlement patterns, my father comments on the ways in which settlers in western Canada adjust to the demands of a multi-cultural society. Since much of the structure of today's lifestyle in western Canada was just emerging when he wrote, many things today complacently taken for granted are foreshadowed in the newsletters printed above.

His observations upon ethnic settlement patterns, for example, foreshadow recent Canadian nationalism and struggles to preserve ethnic identities. He dwells on the specific blends and ways settlers in western Canada adjust to the variety of ethnic, religious, and national backgrounds. He notes, too, that while setters in the western United States were fleeing organized society, in western Canada order came in advance of settlement and the settlers built schools, churches, and libraries — the institutions of organized society.

With the critical faculties of a good journalist and a well-trained social scientist, he both admired and condemned what he saw in North America. The skills, intelligence, and diligence of people and their achievement in making use of the opportunities given them; the intriguing advances built upon older cultural practices from various parts of the world — these things he admired. On the other hand, he condemned the brutal and short-sighted exploitation of resources, human and natural, social and economic.

This contradiction was one which neither he nor others could resolve. When Goethe said, "America you have it better," he was not unaware of the presence of raw, brutal, and violent aspects in the "new world." But his faith in man and the potential of human nature made him optimistic that with the opportunities of this new world would evolve a more humane and culturally rich expression of the best in man. Likewise, my father distinguished civilization, which one could assess in dollars and cents, from culture, an expression of inner values.

Since he was writing essentially for German readers of a German newspaper, it should not surprise us that he wrote of the most successful German settlers, although he did point out that not all German immigrants to Canada became successful farmers. Nor should it surprise us that he also took time to visit Mennonite and Doukhobor settlements in the Canadian West and to comment incisively on their attractive as well as their not-so-attractive aspects. Liberal, well-educated Germans sympathetic to Leo Tolstoi and his friends needed to be informed that many of their views concerning the Doukhobor settlements in the new world were one-sided and unduly optimistic.

Generally, the vividness of his description and discussion of issues comes to us through the people he met — the farm boy who knew a scythe only because he had watched his grandfather use one; the traveller from New York admiring Regina's post office; John Zinkhan, the mason and farmer whose stone house stood solidly on the Saskatchewan prairie; the CPR administrator; the Mennonite teacher; the Nebraska farmer in Alberta; Mormon elders around Lethbridge discussing the economic foundation of their religion. Here, one finds the focus of my father's observations about western Canada. In 1903 he wrote: "For the historian, political power is expressed not merely in ideas but rather in and through people."

Having completed his reports on western Canada, Wilhelm Cohnstaedt returned to Germany and joined the *Frankfurter Zeitung* editorial board in 1910. In 1933 he resigned from his position after refusing to write a compromising editorial about Adolf Hitler's appointment as Prime Minister. After helping to set free his only daughter, who had been arrested by Nazi Stormtroopers, he left for New York and lived in the United States until his death in October 1937. Current historical research records the role he played in the government and politics of the Weimar Republic between 1918 and 1933.

In a more personal note from a son, I would like to add some of my own recollections of my father. I never tired hearing him tell me about the people of past times and places recorded in history. His conversations with me are still vividly impressed on my mind. We travelled together through man's history, social and economic, everywhere in the world. I listened avidly to his accounts of man's journey through life. I remember what an effective public speaker he was — how he used to gesticulate vigorously with his outstretched arms and drive home important points with his hands.

The post-World War I years were turbulent in the aftermath of defeat for Germany. My father took part in the struggles to democratize the country. Using his pen and the spoken word, he expressed himself with moral conviction and a sensitive and humble urbanity. His sense of personal responsibility drove his life into a never-ending search to cope with and to transcend the contradictions in human life. As the purple passages in his prose would indicate, he was in many ways a romantic; yet he trusted his intellect, and he approached each task persistently and rationally.

I am grateful to Herta Holle-Scherer, the translator, for having made these "letters" available to the people of western Canada, among whom are included Wilhelm Cohnstaedt's own grandchildren.

Martin L. Cohnstaedt
University of Regina